Praise for *All In*

"Another power-packed insightful call to leaders to be present, to be the anchor your team needs, Goldsmith, *Only two-time Thinkers 50 #1 Leadership Thinker in the world*

"There can be no effective team without trust. Robb Holman not only makes this point, he also shows us how leaders can generate and integrate trust to their teams to maximize their upside. A very timely and relevant book!" - *Sydney Finkelstein, professor of leadership at Dartmouth College, Author of Bestselling book, Superbosses, and host of The Sydcast*

"If you are serious about building effective teams, don't leave it to chance. *All In* shares actionable strategies for building trust, engagement, and vision in teams at work and in life." - *Ellen Rogin, CPA, CFP(r), Co-Author of the New York Times Bestseller, Picture Your Prosperity*

"In *All In*, Robb Holman gets right to the heart of the matter by reminding us how all teams, whether personal or professional, depend on a level of mutual trust and understanding that cannot be forced upon anyone, but built for the long run carefully, considerately, and intentionally." - *Bryan Falchuk, Bestselling Author and Leadership Expert*

"Leadership presence is essential to an effective team. *All In* provides practical reasoning combined with Holman's no-nonsense tools for instructing leaders how to effectively be with their team." - *Kevin Kruse, CEO, LEADx, and Author of Great Leaders Have No Rules*

"*All In* is the anticipated second effort from conference speaker, business coach, and influence expert, Robb Holman. His straightforward approach aims at the heart of effective team leadership, the presence of the leader themselves. Not for the timid, rather those seeking the higher levels." - *Cy Wakeman, Drama Researcher and New York Times Bestselling Author of No Ego*

"Too often there's a lack of accountability from leaders who complain that team members are not engaged enough. What so few realize is that real engagement starts with the leader themselves going *All In*. In Robb Holman's book, he walks readers through the practical steps to not only go all in, but also have your team members come with you!" - *Dov Baron, Inc Top 100 Leadership Speaker, Multiple Bestselling Author, Top 30 Global Leadership Gurus, Host of the #1 Podcast to make you a better leader (Inc.com)*

"...The ability to connect personal stories and experiences seamlessly to relatable and practical best practices within the workplace is an art form. Robb Holman provides us with a laser-focused lens in *All In* to zoom in and decode how to build trust and make it last...."- *Lou Diamond, Keynote Speaker, Bestselling Author, and CEO of Thrive*

"*All In* adeptly converts the concept of team trust into concrete actions. This empowers us to elevate our personal and team effectiveness. A powerful tool for work and home!" - *Lee J. Colan, Ph.D., Author of The Power of Positive Coaching*

"*All In* is a step-by-step guide to build a solid foundation for a thriving team. By following the simple but powerful principles in the book, you'll lead teams with empowered individuals who collaborate harmoniously to achieve their goals." - *Cloris Kylie, Bestselling Author of Beyond Influencer Marketing*

"Robb Holman hits the nail on the head. If you want stronger teams and cultures that win together, *All In* should be your go-to manifesto." - *Marcel Schwantes, Founder and Chief Human Officer of Leadership from the Core*

"Robb is a true student of leadership. This comes through in a powerful way within the pages of *All In*." - *John Eades, Author of Building the Best*

"Trust is foundational to leadership. Robb Holman's newest book, *All In* shows why trust is important and how you can develop it as a means of leading more effectively." - *John Baldoni, Inc.com Top 50 Leadership Expert, Executive Coach and Author of more than a dozen books on leadership*

"Robb makes essential leadership skills practical and actionable with engaging stories and research. Read this book if you want to take your team to the next level." - *Dan Rockwell, Inc Magazine Top 50 Leadership Expert and Author of the Leadership Freak Blog*

All iN

HOW IMPACTFUL TEAMS BUILD TRUST FROM THE INSIDE OUT

ROBB HOLMAN

ISBN: 978-1-4834-6157-1 (sc)
ISBN: 978-1-4834-6674-3 (e)

Lulu Publishing Services rev. date: 09/27/2019

I dedicate this book to the best team player I have ever known, my wife, Karen Holman. Karen, you have demonstrated what impactful teamwork is all about through your continued love, trust, and perseverance. We truly make a great team!

In addition, I acknowledge my parents, June Wright and Bob Holman. You have modeled that through family diversity, you can remain a unified front through forgiveness, hope, and love.

Next, I acknowledge my *All In* team who has provided a strong sense of encouragement, creativity, and diligence to this very important project. Thanks to Brianna Johnson, Fred Balliet, Rob Lehman, Anne Tanswai, Thomas Schliep, and Muhammad Asim.

Lastly, I acknowledge all of the foundational team members who have strategically partnered with me throughout the years. Thanks Scott Holman, Phil Carnuccio, Fred Balliet, Frank Foy, David Sill, Todd Rogers, Justin Crawford, and Ryan Gerardi. You have demonstrated courage, selflessness, and a willingness to explore together.

CONTENTS

FOREWORD

Robb and I became friends after his appearance on my *LEADx Leadership* podcast for the release of his first book, *Lead the Way*. Since then, our synergy and shared passion for impactful leadership has grown more and more evident.

Robb's vivacious spirit and ability to get straight to the heart of the matter makes this follow up book both inspiring and motivating.

As an entrepreneur since the age of 22, I've come to know the distinct difference between effective and lackluster leadership. Effective leadership permeates all other aspects of life, even influencing your family relationships. This is true for each and every person on your team. *All In* doesn't hide from this reality, but instead provides instruction, poignant stories, and advice that helps you cultivate strong professional bonds from the inside out.

All In potently addresses the employee engagement epidemic many organizations are currently up against.

After two failed business ventures, I changed the most important aspect of my career – myself. I embarked on the path of heart-centered leadership and genuine productivity and have since built and sold several multimillion-dollar companies.

The difference lies in *how* you lead. Breakthroughs happen when we learn to build *trust*.

I can say with absolute confidence that the *Inside Out Leadership* principles Robb outlines in this book will walk you down the path of creating the business you always envisioned. With practical exercises, intelligent concepts, and a sprinkle of humor, Robb shows how he personally laid the groundwork for his own inside out enterprises – And exactly how you can do the same with your team by your side.

You'll find that *All In* not only illustrates the modern problems leaders face, but it defines why they exist and how to transform them in actionable steps.

Kevin Kruse
Author of *Great Leaders Have No Rules*
CEO, LEADx
www.LEADx.org

INTRODUCTION

IN 2017, THE ASSOCIATION OF MBAs and The Game Changer Index conducted a three-month survey asking 865 industry-diverse leaders to name issues that lead to breakdowns in team collaboration. The study revealed that the top two causes of team breakdown are *poor leadership* and *poor communication* between team members. Overwhelmingly, the top cause was poor leadership, as nearly 70% of respondents said that it had been a factor in collaboration breakdown in the past year.

Sadly, my 22 years as an international executive coach, trainer, and speaker has told me a similar story.

If we want to foster more impactful team dynamics, it starts with YOU as the leader. The more effective you are, the more effective your team will ultimately be.

In my 2017 book, *Lead the Way* (www.LeadTheWayBook.com), I guided readers into their hearts to lead themselves in a more effective and fulfilling way. Now, I am revealing how leaders can bolster and transform the work of their entire team.

In order to experience this kind of team transformation, *trust* is the key that unlocks *impactful leadership* and *healthy communication*! If you don't have trust, you don't have anything.

All In takes you on an inspirational and practical journey of learning *how* to build trust from the inside out. When trust is built from the inside out, teams can accomplish the impossible together!

When you are committed to building trust with team members who are different from you, transformation occurs within ourselves, our families, our businesses, our communities, and the world.

Are you READY to go *All In*?

Robb Holman
Holman International
Founder & Chief Inspiration Officer
www.robbholman.com

PART I

Connecting And Connection

CHAPTER 1

Building Trust that Lasts

"A healthy relationship is built on unwavering trust." - Beau Mirchoff

ONE OF THE MOST TRANSFORMATIVE moments of my life was in my first year of marriage. Karen and I were driving back from a friend's wedding in Tennessee. Hours stretched ahead of us in the long drive back to Pennsylvania. Tension was mounting after a major conflict the night before, and it was one of the quietest rides of my entire life.

Have you ever been in a situation where the silence was deafening? Imagine that for several hours.

Then, out of nowhere, my own words surprised me.

"We need help."

The moment I blurted it out, I thought I had failed. I believed I had failed my wife, our marriage, and myself. I certainly didn't want to become yet another divorce statistic, and I knew something needed to change - Me!

Little did I know, these three words became the most powerful words I had ever spoken. They opened up the doors to the path that saved my marriage. In the homestretch of our trip home, Karen and I had a meaningful and timely conversation in which we both committed to marriage counseling.

Basically, I was trying to transform Karen into someone like me, and she was doing the same thing. We were assuming that things would only get easier if we could change the other person. I remember praying on multiple occasions, *"God, will you change Karen to become more like me so that our marriage can be more unified?!"*

Just as a marriage needs two healthy participants, companies need team members to be the healthiest versions of themselves - offering unique perspectives on situations, people, challenges, and opportunities as they arise. *This* builds trust. In Chapter 6, we'll talk more about conflict resolution.

The Story Behind the Story

Entering into marriage, Karen and I had a solid foundation of trust. Well, at least I thought we did. We believed we were anchored in trust, but our foundation was shakier than we knew.

Looking back, I didn't truly know what trust meant, let alone how to build and foster it. I am the offspring of two parents who loved each other but ultimately couldn't make their marriage work. They divorced when I was in high school. This took a big toll on the sensitive and peace-loving kid that I was. All that I knew about trust was damaged from that point on. Up until my marital challenges, I had shoved down this confusion, hurt, and pain, assuming that time would heal all wounds.

But it didn't.

The pain kept finding its way out and affecting my relationships. It especially impacted my relationship with Karen, who was closest to me. On top of this, Karen had her own unresolved issues about her father, who passed away suddenly when she was in college. We were two different people coming from two different homes who had experienced unique dysfunction.

Research shows that our experience is not uncommon.

According to The American Psychological Association, *"In Western cultures, more than 90 percent of people marry by age 50. Healthy marriages are good for couples' mental and physical health. They are also good for children; growing up in a happy home protects children from mental, physical, educational and social problems. However, about 40 to 50 percent of married couples in the United States divorce. The divorce rate for subsequent marriages is even higher."*

In her 2016 Huffington Post article, *The Connection Between Childhood Experiences and Adult Problems*, Marcia Sirota explains the impact that the home has on children:

"Every person who's walked through my office door suffering from depression, anxiety, relationship or work problems, low self-esteem, or addiction has a history of some type of adversity in their childhood. It's become clear to me by listening to their stories that, were it not for these painful events, the person wouldn't be struggling as much as they are today. It's become abundantly clear over the past 20-plus years of doing psychotherapy that childhood experiences are at the root of adult problems."

We pass on our learned behaviors without even realizing it. If there is dysfunction in the home between two or more people, young children pick up on it and begin acting out those behaviors. **As human beings, we do what we have experienced.**

Even in cases where people swear to never repeat what they experienced as children, they often end up repeating patterns in ways they never expected. For example, if someone experiences abuse as a child they may vow to never become an abuser. But they may find themselves married to an abusive partner years later.

And we wonder why professional team dynamics are so dysfunctional. If we are to truly grasp why teams at home and at work are failing, it comes down to one key factor: a lack of trust. Think about it - a lack of commitment, unhealthy conflicts, a muddled vision, etc. - All are byproducts of a bond that was either broken or never forged.

If teams are not functioning in a vibrant and sustainable way, people are going to emotionally and/or physically 'cut the cord.' They're going to check out.

If you don't have trust you don't have anything.

In order to overcome this systemic problem in our homes, workplaces, and the world in which we live, one thing is certain: We need the awareness and courage to unlearn old patterns and commit to new ones. That's what this book is all about!

Rebuilding Our Foundation of Trust

In retrospect, that challenging car ride was one of the best things that could've ever happened to Karen and I. It made us boldly aware of the trust issues we both needed to acknowledge.

We met with a highly recommended marriage counselor until our foundation of trust was solid. As a result, Karen and I have enjoyed a vibrant and healthy marriage for more than fifteen years, three amazing kids, and a bedrock of trust that continues to deepen every day.

You might be thinking, *"What does this have to do with my team?"*

Teams are all around us. At home, in our hobbies, and certainly in the workplace. Maybe it's not a long, awkward car ride with your spouse, but a subtle disagreement with a team member that is wreaking havoc on your peace of mind.

Could there be something deeper going on within you? Within them?

People are often triggered by old wounds in both minor and major workplace disagreements because their trust was already broken long ago. And so the patterns repeat themselves until we recognize them for what they are.

When people rub us the wrong way, say or do something to undermine the relationship, or control us with impure motives, it damages trust.

Trust must come before anything else. In order to better understand how to build and foster trust with team members, we must learn more about trust.

So what is trust and where does it come from?

The Merriam-Webster Dictionary defines trust as the "assured reliance on the character, ability, strength, or truth of someone or something."

One factor that stands out from my marriage story is presence. Karen and I spend time together not so that we can get something from the other. Instead, we share life experience that is mutually beneficial.

Before we sought counseling, we thought we were relying on one another, but we were actually relying more on ourselves. My own past wounds had me trying to change Karen to become who I wanted her to be. These old wounds were obstacles keeping me from being present, and so I spent more time reacting than responding. As a result, I had unhealthy and unfair expectations that set Karen up for failure. The pattern fed my insecurities and an unwillingness to invest in the relationship.

With this *outside in* approach, we were missing one another. I was trying to change her to meet my needs instead of changing myself to meet her needs. This cycle continued until we committed to working through our insecurities from the inside out. As a result, we learned how to feel assured and rely on each other.

As we became aware of negative patterns and healed from our past experiences, we embarked upon an *inside out* lifestyle that taught us how to be truly present in our marriage.

Think of a time when you were with someone, perhaps a team member, who was completely undistracted. They were giving their undivided attention to you. In a sense, they made you feel as if you were the only person on earth. How did it make you feel?

Valued? Honored? Respected? Loved? Appreciated?

Presence is powerful. It is not self-seeking. It does not think about the next meeting, the leaky faucet that needs fixing, or the next creative idea. When you are present, the rest of the world fades away beyond that one-on-one interaction. It's a grand opportunity to get to know the other person. As you get more acquainted, you get a feel for the character, ability, and truth of that person. This is where the foundation of trust, which builds credibility, begins.

How to Build (or Re-Build) a Foundation of Trust

So much in leadership comes down to how you build trust, but companies are often overly concerned with numbers. They care about *how much* is built, but not *how* it is built.

It's common for companies to focus on how many people they employ, how many core team members they have, how many businesses they've started, or how much revenue they've made. Since mainstream business culture is obsessed with numbers, these factors can easily become badges of honor.

As a lifelong serial entrepreneur, I've had the pleasure of starting many for-profit and nonprofit organizations over the last 22 years. In this time, I've discovered that true success isn't based on how many people join your team. It's based on the level of depth you share with each person.

Having devoted team members is the result of developing strong personal relationships. This 'slow is fast' method of team-building may not bear fruit overnight, but in the long run, both your team and company will thrive.

Imagine what would happen if we learned how to redirect our energy (time, resources, focus, etc.) away from unnecessary meetings and toward real human exchange?

We will reach the masses if we reach the one.

This kind of perspective is counter-intuitive for most leaders because it requires swimming against the current of our culture. Sadly, American culture focuses on reaching the masses while largely ignoring the individual. As a result, team and business relationships are failing on a grand scale.

"About 60% of the time, work teams fail to accomplish their goals," according to Dr. Eunice Parisi-Carew, a Founding Associate at The Ken Blanchard Companies. "To make matters worse, the experience will create lingering hard feelings among team members."

In his Harvard Business Review article, professor and author Behnam Tabrizi's findings were equally dismal: "In a detailed study of 95 teams in 25 leading corporations, chosen by an independent panel of academics and experts, I found that nearly 75% of cross-functional teams are dysfunctional."

In light of this glaring problem, let's take a deeper dive into some of the reasons why teams fail.

Respected leadership expert and consultant, Patrick Lencioni says, "If we don't trust one another, then we aren't going to engage in open, constructive, ideological conflict. And we'll just continue to preserve a sense of artificial harmony." In his best-selling book, *The Five Dysfunctions of a Team*, he makes a strong research and experiential argument that the

#1 source of dysfunction in teams is a lack of trust. Lencioni provides the following juxtaposition:

Members of teams with an absence of trust...	Members of trusting teams...
✓ Conceal their weaknesses and mistakes from one another	✓ Admit weaknesses and mistakes
✓ Hesitate to ask for help or provide constructive feedback	✓ Ask for help
✓ Hesitate to offer help outside their own areas of responsibility	✓ Accept questions and input about their areas of responsibility
✓ Jump to conclusions about the intentions and aptitudes of others without attempting to clarify them	✓ Give one another the benefit of the doubt before arriving at a negative conclusion
✓ Fail to recognize and tap into one another's skills and experiences	✓ Take risks in offering feedback and assistance ✓ Appreciate and tap into one another's skills and experiences
✓ Hold grudges	✓ Focus time and energy on important issues, not politics ✓ Offer and accept apologies without hesitation
✓ Dread meetings and find reasons to avoid spending time together	✓ Look forward to meetings and other opportunities to work as a group

There is hope for building trust that lasts.

One of the greatest ways to relearn trust is to surround yourself with teams that have a strong bond. In any healthy and unified relationship, you will find an unwavering, enduring trust.

The Philadelphia Eagles finally won a Super Bowl in 2018 after a magical season. As a Philadelphia-area native, I must say it was a bit like heaven on earth when we beat the New England Patriots and won our first Super Bowl in franchise history.

A team that suffered so many trials, tribulations, and doubts still pulled off one of the greatest seasons and championship games in NFL history. Following their big win, a lot of people asked me what I thought was the single most important factor that led to their success.

Certainly, I could point to any number of assets that played an important role in their victory. Things like the spiritual dynamic, synergy of the coaches and players, willingness to overcome obstacles, receptivity to the overall shared vision, and many more!

However, in learning about some of the practical implementations of the coaching staff, I gained keen insight into a foundational principle. Doug Peterson set intentional and consistent times for players to get to know one another, not as professionals, but as people. During these meetups, the players heard each other's life stories (a topic we'll delve into in Chapter 3), which was a perfect opportunity to build trust. The players got to know each other as real people with real journeys, weaknesses, obstacles, and hearts that beat with a common love of football.

The average team member (and human being) wants to be valued. One of the best ways to demonstrate value is to set aside time to be with someone. Time provides the opportunity to accept, understand, and appreciate another person - but that's not all.

A Valuable Lesson Learned from My Son

Early one morning before everyone else was awake, I asked my 10-year-old, RJ, a question. The situation wasn't unusual, as he and I are the 'early birds' of the family who love to start each day with a time of gratitude. The question was one that I didn't want to ask, but I knew that doing so would help me understand him on a whole new level.

"RJ, do you think Dad is on his phone too much when he is with you and the family?"

He quickly responded, "Yes, Dad! You know you're on the phone a lot, right?"

I was cut to my core. It was something I already knew, but hearing it from my son broke my heart.

I continued by asking, "How does that make you feel?"

His response hit me at a depth I didn't know was possible.

"When you talk on the phone when we're around, it makes me feel like you care about them more than us."

In that moment my eyes welled up with tears and I said, "I'm so sorry buddy. Will you forgive me?"

Shortly after this intimate and vulnerable exchange with my boy, I heard the rest of my family coming down the stairs. I gathered everyone in the kitchen and explained my exchange with RJ. I asked if this was how everyone else felt, and sadly, it was. I openly apologized and asked for forgiveness from the entire family.

This story highlights a fascinating truth about trust: It is not built when things are easy. Instead, it's how you respond in the face of challenges and tough questions that arise within your team.

When we live lives of transparency, there are opportunities for relational trust that would have never occurred otherwise. We will talk more about this and healthy conflict resolution in Chapter 6.

One of the ways we form trust is by learning how to engage in healthy communication. In Chapter 2, we'll discuss this more deeply.

Reflection and Rating

Are you living more *outside in* or *inside out* as a team member? As we discussed, the former has a 'build it and they will come' mentality, while the latter is being present with others and building them up.

On a scale from 1 to 10 (1: not doing it at all, 10: doing it all the time), how often would you say you are present with your team members?

Now, what is one thing you are willing to commit to over the next 30 days to have more presence with your team?

CHAPTER 2

Communication – What's in It for Them Is What's in It for You

"The art of communication is the language of leadership." -
James Humes

AFTER CHAPTER 1, YOU MIGHT be thinking:

Can team members really be that complex?

I didn't sign up for trying to understand my own wounds, patterns, and dysfunctions, let alone my team members'!

Does having this awareness of past hurts mean I should get counseling to be more present?

….and many more!

It's normal to have different questions, thoughts, and opinions at this point. I always encourage leaders and team members to continue the *inside out* process to see what surfaces for them.

We have discussed how presence is a critical component of building trust. As we devote more intentional and consistent time with team members, knowing how to best connect with them becomes equally important.

Change and Mutual Benefit

We live in a world of crazy schedules, demands, and responsibilities, both personally and professionally. In case you haven't noticed, it doesn't look like the world is slowing down any time soon.

Consider team members who have multiple kids in extracurricular activities during the week, or a team member who is biting off more than they can chew in an attempt to help another struggling team member.

It's a simple fact that the average professional is bombarded with more obligations, responsibilities, and opportunities than they know what to do with. Like it or not, people are generally self-centered, but that doesn't mean people are selfish. It simply means that anything or anyone that brings change into their life must benefit them in some way. Otherwise, they are resistant.

In order to build trust and know how to foster relationships that will bring an element of change to your life, it is imperative to consider WIIFM.

I love what Roger Dean Duncan said in his Fast Company article, *In Times Of Change, "What's In It For Me?" Is The Question You Need To Answer*:

"When confronted with change, most people tune in to their favorite internal radio station: WIIFM—What's In It For Me? It's not that most people are selfish. It's simply that personal context is usually the first filter we use to evaluate our environment. It's especially true when we're asked to participate in some sort of change.

What am I losing? Where are we headed? What will the new place look like? How will it be different from what I have now? What about the work flow? Who will be my teammates? What will be expected of me? What performance metrics will be used?

In other words, what's in it for me?"

Connection Is Looking After the Interest of Others

When we recognize what's in it for the other person, we can take a proactive step. We can serve and take a sincere interest in them. From here, we can discover that what's in it for them is *also* what's in it for us.

To fully engage in this process, we need proactive communication. If we master this skill, imagine how much more effectively we can deepen our relationships with others.

Case in point: There are two different approaches business leaders take when they participate in a networking event. The first leader heads in with as many business cards as possible, eager to hand out as many cards to as many people as possible. The hope is that the more cards they hand out, the more calls they will receive. Then they wait, wait, and wait some more for the phone to ring, or for the email to appear. Only once in a great while do they strike gold, and the cycle continues.

In comes the second leader with a very different approach. They actually come ready to meet people - They don't bring any business cards with them. Instead of feeling bad about not handing out any cards, they see it as an opportunity. This leader is intentional about getting *other people's* business cards. They take a proactive step to get in touch with people they meet rather than anxiously awaiting a call that may never come.

Do you see this subtle All In approach that makes a world of difference? It's acting as though the ball is in someone else's court vs. acting like it is in your own.

Let's take the bull by the horns and foster proactive communication.

We may not always be collecting business cards, but we always have chances to intentionally connect with the greatest of life's gifts - people!

As a professional public speaker for more than 20 years and a highly social person, I have discovered some proven communication strategies that will help you connect with others from the inside out. When we embrace these 5 proactive communication principles, we see how *what's in it for them is also what's in it for us.*

Embrace Silence

I can't help but think that when Karen and I first started dating, there was nothing worse than 'dead air' in conversation. Before our dates, I would think through an exhaustive list of things that I could potentially ask her. The problem was, I had to remember what I had already asked her so I wouldn't repeat myself! Any hint of lethargy in our conversations felt awkward, uncomfortable, and sometimes downright scary.

Well, no matter how hard I prepared, as the extrovert of extroverts that I am, the conversation would inevitably lull for a few seconds (which felt like a few hours).

Can I get an amen? I'm assuming in my vulnerability that I'm not alone, so it makes it much more humorous.

Since those early days, Karen and I have slowly but surely forged a platform of trust that has liberated us from these unnecessary worries. Now, some of the sweetest times are when we are sitting together and completely embracing the silence. Our mere presence together is enough. No need to speak; no need to act.

I believe the reason this can be so challenging is that people don't get a chance to breathe anymore. We place so many expectations on ourselves and one another. Not to mention, American culture equates all activity as good activity, and this cannot be further from the truth.

We need to learn to slow down and move past the fear that silence and stillness is not ok. Not only is it ok, but we need it to be effective in any relationship.

Connecting like this with a team member will happen naturally over time as your trust grows. Here are a couple of key points to remember:

1) Embrace silence in the midst of any line of communication. The more comfortable you are with silence, the more others will be too.

2) When you embrace silence, you can begin to let the moment sink in and be more sensitive and discerning. Where to go, what to do, and how to say something will become clearer.

Create Active Participation

When I facilitate my interactive training series, *Public Speaking Is Much Easier Than You Think,* I often share that I have seen studies that rank the fear of public speaking over death.

I love comedian Jerry Seinfeld's take on this: *"According to most studies, people's number one fear is public speaking. Number two is death. Death is number two. Does that seem right? That means to the average person, if you have to go to a funeral, you're better off in the casket than doing the eulogy."*

Since this is a reality for a lot of people, I like to demystify some things about public speaking to encourage participants of my training series.

One idea many people pick up over the years is that speaking in front of any number of people means we have to entertain them. In other words, as soon as it's showtime, they must put on some kind of dog and pony show. This couldn't be further from the truth.

I believe one of the main culprits of this idea (at least in the Western World) is consumerism. We have been swept up in a culture of creating passive consumers rather than active participants. There seems to be an almost gravitational pull toward, and a pressure to be, the life of the party at all times.

This is dangerous for reasons we discussed in the last chapter - so much depends upon *how* we build our organizations.

Are you building around you or beyond you? In other words, are you building around your personality, or an exchange between two human beings resulting in equal net value? I will talk more about this concept in Chapter 7.

When you meet with a person or group and feel pressured to perform, share in that spotlight. Then, it's not about you, or even the others, but your *exchange*. Both of you together! Have fun and be creative in this process.

One of the simple, impactful, and practical things I've learned about creating active participation is the art of asking good questions.

If you are meeting someone for the first time, begin by asking about their life journey. What milestones led them to where they are? For a team member who you already know, make it a point to learn something new about them every time you meet.

Asking great questions gets people talking about themselves and opening up in a very natural way. Before long, people are chatting about other interests and topics with which you can *connect*. As we make a concerted effort in getting to know each other, space opens up for each person to share. Now *this* is active participation!

As we learn to intentionally take a deeper dive in personal and professional conversation, there is something else to keep in mind. This next communication tool will help you continue to bolster trust and ignite proactive communication.

The Art of Storytelling

What's your favorite movie and what's the storyline?

Mine has to be *Good Will Hunting*. What can I say, I'm a sucker for relationship-driven movies and this one is a diamond!

Will Hunting (Matt Damon) has a genius-level IQ but chooses to work as a janitor at MIT. When he solves a complex graduate-level math problem, his talents are uncovered by Professor Gerald Lambeau (Stellan Skarsgard), who decides to help the misguided youth reach his potential. When Will is arrested for attacking a police officer, Professor Lambeau makes a deal to get leniency for him if he will receive treatment from therapist Sean Maguire (Robin Williams). Because of his troubled past, Will struggles to have authentic relationships and is afraid to open up to new possibilities. That is, until his therapist helps him overcome his demons and heal the fractured parts of his life.

Storytelling is woven into the fabric of our culture and is passed down through generations. It seems that everywhere we turn, there are stories grabbing our attention, whether inspirational or disturbing.

Thought-provoking stories make up our media, interesting stories find space on digital and physical bookshelves, and Hollywood has made billions of dollars off of brilliant storylines. Not to mention, many organizations owe a significant amount of their growth to a compelling story.

So if stories are all around us making an impact, shouldn't we know how to tell a good story? If we want to know how to share great stories with our team, it begins by knowing how to tell your personal story. You will learn more about this in the next chapter!

Be Yourself

In 2017, I released my first book, *Lead the Way*. The big idea behind the book is that when we go on a self-discovery journey to uncover our unique seeds of greatness, it awakens our personal purpose. When our personal purpose is ignited, our professional life is infused with this new sense of purpose. We are much more engaged!

In *Lead the Way*, I talk about the comparison trap. So many of us walk around exerting conscious and subconscious energy comparing ourselves to others. I call it the "If I Syndrome."

"If I had more money like Bob, If I had a marriage like my neighbor's marriage, If I had Pam's looks, If I had Jill's influence, If I had Jim's connections..."

This is a draining pattern that debilitates us over time.

Learning to be comfortable in your own skin, regardless of where you are and what you are doing, is one of the most liberating experiences in the world. If you want to understand who you are, here are 5 questions leaders should ask themselves (borrowed from my *Discover Your Life Purpose* tool):

1. *Do you know your personal core values?* These are values in which you stand firm. They are strong convictions of the heart, as I like to call them.
2. *What are your top strengths?* These are the things that come easy to you. They don't require as much hard work, and they are fruitful.
3. *What are the top passions in your life?* These are things that literally have you leaping out of bed in the morning. They can be work or pleasure-related. You could easily talk about or engage in these activities all day long.
4. *What are your top life milestones?* These are things that have helped make you into the person you are today. It could be the divorce of a family member. It could be the birth of your first child. It could be your first job or your first entrepreneurial paycheck. Whether it was a joyous or a challenging experience, a stake was put in the ground either way. Maybe you didn't fully understand it at the time, but a part of you knew you would never be the same. Milestones are about owning your story, and in that process, helping others own their stories.
5. *What's the primary gift you've been given?* There may be some crossover between strengths, passions, and gifts, but a gift isn't as much for you as it is for others. Your gifts impact and influence others. For instance, are you gifted at encouraging people? Are you super compassionate? Are you a gifted leader? Great at solving complex problems? When you understand your primary gift,

you can then present it to others who unwrap those gifts, so to speak. It's a legacy you leave behind that can even affect future generations.

So these are the five areas that help affirm and clarify who you are. And we must know ourselves deeply in order to genuinely connect with anyone else. This leads us to the next logical question, "*Why* am I actually here?"

When you're truly living life on purpose, you start to communicate from a deep conviction. Those that speak from the mind get mental responses from others, while those that speak from the heart get hearts on fire!

Every healthy relationship requires both parties to take a step toward each other. As you are better equipped to take our proactive communication steps, you begin to connect with other team members. This is your intentional steps toward them.

Now it's time to have them take a step toward you in this mutual exchange of connection. The languages of appreciation will help you serve them in this process.

Understand the Language of Appreciation

Psychologist and philosopher William James said, *"The deepest principle of human nature is a craving to be appreciated."*

Even as we button up and step foot in the workplace, this truth still applies. The more we understand how our team members want and need to be appreciated, the faster we will create trust and establish credibility.

The Five Love Languages was a #1 New York Times bestselling book in 1995. Written by Gary Chapman, the book outlines 5 ways people express and experience love: receiving or experiencing gifts, quality time, words of affirmation, acts of service, and physical touch. After years of counseling couples as a church pastor, Chapman concludes that these emotional languages allow people to express and understand love.

Now I know what some of you are thinking - Come on, Robb! How does this sappy stuff apply in the workplace?

Well, in 2017 Chapman teamed up with Paul White to write *The 5 Languages of Appreciation in the Workplace.* The follow-up book takes the love languages and applies them to the workplace.

I like how Ashley Faus summarizes it in her *Daily Muse* article, *The 5 Love Languages: Office Edition*:

"Like it or not, your job is kind of like a romantic relationship. The premise of the 5 Love Languages—that there's no one-size-fits-all approach to showing others that you care—is also pretty invaluable advice when you're trying to attract a new customer, strengthen a client relationship, or keep your co-workers happy. Everyone's different, so the key is finding out which type of attention makes your colleagues and clients feel most valued."

If you want more trusting relationships with team members, it starts with you. It requires *you* to be present. The most effective way for you to be present is by practicing connection with others. This is where proactive communication comes in - It's the best way to serve others. Remember: what's in it for them is what's in it for me.

The 5 proactive communication principles we discussed that help you serve from the inside out are: Embrace Silence, Create Active

Participation, Use Storytelling, Be Yourself, and Understand the Languages of Appreciation.

Reflection

Consider the last time you did something thoughtful for a team member.

Which love language would it fall under - gift giving, quality time, words of affirmation, acts of service, or physical touch? Whether it's an impromptu meetup (quality time), a kind handshake (physical touch), or praise for a job well done (words of affirmation), these communication styles reveal our preferences.

Make a list of important team members and reflect on a time when each one revealed which language they prefer.

Who is one team member you can serve more intentionally in the next 30 days with one or more of these communication principles?

Chapter 3
Embracing the Story

"Every person on this planet has a story to tell, something that makes them unique adding to the whole." - Madisyn Taylor

ONE OF THE MOST POWERFUL communication principles we discussed last chapter is the art of storytelling, and I felt compelled to dig deeper into this concept. So let's go!

A fundamental quality of humans is that we all want to feel like we are on a journey with others, not alone. This extraordinary desire to bond is what makes us human, and as we discussed back in Chapter 1, it creates an opportunity for presence.

One thing many of you may not know is that my mom is an artist and one of the most creative people I know. Not just creative on canvas, but also in what she has taught me about perspective.

For years, I always admired my mom's finished work. Whether it was a mural, canvas painting, or sculpture, I always waited with anticipation to see the finished piece - until a few years ago. I stopped by while she was in the middle of a painting project. It was as though I had entered a war zone of color. Sketched images were strewn all over the place. To be honest, I didn't know whether to run or hide!

For the first time, I asked her questions about a half-finished piece.

"Why are you using those colors?"

"Why are you painting a face like that?"

What caused you to think through a scene like that?"

I started to learn more about what was moving my mom to make the decisions she did. I am so grateful that she took the time to answer my questions and involve me in the story she was telling.

I came away from this wonderful bonding and learning process with invaluable lessons that enhanced my perspective on life and leadership:

1. Ralph Waldo Emerson was spot on with his quote, *"It's not the destination, it's the journey."*
2. Every human being (whether they fully realize it or not) longs to share their story with others.
3. By sharing in my mom's journey, I helped shape the destination of her project.
4. My mom's creative process proves how impactful *inside out* living can be. We can share our experiences and create a mutual benefit.

The average person loves to talk about him or herself.

Whenever I sit down with someone for the first time I say, "Tell me your story!" In professional meetings, this catches some people off guard because they expect a professional, surface-level conversation, or they expect to simply dive into the task at hand. The truth is that I care more about the person than what they do. That doesn't mean I don't care about what they do; it just means that I have things in the proper order. When you place people before things, it is always an opportunity to foster trust.

When we can learn some of a person's story, it gives us a much better understanding of who they are and what led them to where they are now.

I don't just do this the first time. If the opportunity presents itself, I try to find out something new about a person each time I meet with them.

Everyone Should Get to Tell Their Story

Have you ever been around someone who claims to want to know all about you, only to run up the time clock telling their own story? On occasion, you might also meet someone who wants to know all about you while avoiding telling any of their story. They may want to keep the attention on you so that you never really find out who they are. But genuine relationship is always about both parties - learning about one another and witnessing that growth over time.

Sharing personal stories is about making *connection points* in which you can build a natural bridge from the personal into the professional without it being weird or awkward. As we embrace stories, they become like chain links that join us together in a multitude of ways. The more links we create, the stronger and more complex our bonds become.

So, tell me your story!

...Ok, I'll go first.

My Story

I grew up in a small town in Pennsylvania called Chester Springs with my parents, an older brother, and a younger sister. Our farmhouse, built in 1779, was surrounded by 10 acres. As a middle child, I was a sensitive, happy-go-lucky peacemaker who enjoyed playing sports and hanging out with friends. Our Christian faith was the fabric of our lives, and we experienced a lot together as a family. I remember traveling internationally three different times as a teenager. My dad was a family business owner, and my mom was a stay-at-home parent turned business owner herself. (I know what you're thinking - This is where Robb gets it from!)

Though we all loved each other deeply, we were far from a perfect family. As most families do, we had our fair share of dysfunction. From the outside, things probably appeared to be more perfect than they actually were. My parents separated when I was a teenager and eventually got divorced after my junior year of high school. I'm very grateful for outlets like sports, counselors, and some good old-fashioned fun with friends. My faith provided a much-needed anchor, and my hobbies served as a much-needed escape.

It was around this time that college basketball teams began to take notice of me. Soon after, the letters were flowing in, coaches were visiting, and I was preparing for college visitations to see what team and university would be the best fit for my family and I. After a few different visits, I found my home at Widener University, a small private school right outside of Philadelphia. As a freshman, I had the amazing opportunity to make an impact on my team almost immediately.

Throughout my four years of college, I had my ups and downs as most do in that season of life. By sophomore year, I declared Business Administration as my major, saw a considerable amount of playing time on the basketball court, and felt really good about my inner circle of friends on campus. Overall, things were going well, and I was getting acclimated to the college scene - at least it looked that way!

Little did people know, this carefree kid who wore his heart on his sleeve was hurting deep down inside. Still melancholy over my parents' divorce and subsequent remarriages during the summer after my freshman year of college, I was just trying to make sense of the world around me. Change is the word that best described my life at that time, but all I really wanted was stability. It was not unlike me to take long walks late at night only to find myself behind buildings crying out to God to make sense of it all. After an hour or so of crying and wrestling with questions, I would clean myself up, walk back to my dorm room, and act as if nothing ever happened.

Fast forward to the summer before my senior year. I was 21 and ready to embark on the best year of my life. At least, that's what I thought - senior year, business student, captain of a national NCAA basketball team. People assumed I was on top of the world. Yet secretly, I had been rocked by some bad news. There was a mass in my midsection that had gone undiagnosed for nearly a month and a half. I missed most of the pre-season basketball training and was still struggling with my parents' divorce and other problems. It was like everything had come to a head. I was overwhelmed, my body was obviously breaking down, and I was questioning my spiritual life, as God felt so distant. Hurt and confused, I shut down.

Now I've got to be honest with you. Leading up to this point, purpose for me was drinking with friends on the weekends and winning the next basketball game. That's what got me out of bed in the morning. But after being hit with this baffling diagnosis, I began asking questions that I'd never asked before.

What does my life even mean?

Doctors feared that the mass was cancerous. It was so unusual that the medical specialists had never seen anything like it. I was given scan after scan, MRI after MRI, and several ultrasounds. The "best of the best" specialists didn't know what it was, and even worse, they didn't know how to treat it!

Like many people suddenly faced with the unknown, I came to grips with the worst-case scenario.

I have cancer, and I'm going to die.

The thought kept running through my head.

Finally, someone suggested I meet with an ultrasound specialist who I had not yet seen at the University of Pennsylvania Hospital. I braced for more bad news, but as he examined me, he couldn't believe what he saw.

"I can't explain it, but what you had coming in, you don't have any longer."

I was dumbfounded. *Did I hear him correctly?*

He said, "Look. I'm going to show you the ultrasound screen, so pay close attention."

At that moment I perked up and my eyes locked onto the screen. We both scanned the screen up and down, left and right, but saw absolutely nothing. The mass was gone. It was a modern day miracle.

The experience radically altered my perspective. The best way I can describe the feeling is like spiritual fireworks going off in the depths of my being. Instantly, purpose went from winning the next basketball game to, "I'm alive for a reason, and I gotta find out what that reason is!"

This milestone catalyzed a transformation in me. I began viewing people and things from a higher perspective. I was overjoyed to finish my 4th year of college strong, finishing with a BS in Business Administration, a captain position on one of the most successful basketball teams in Widener's history, and steadily improving family relationships.

Shortly after I graduated, the entrepreneurial juices were flowing. But people were telling me that my basketball skills were better suited for the professional leagues. So I was invited to a pro basketball training camp in the Atlantic Basketball Association (ABA).

During this time, I found myself applying for some entry level marketing jobs only to discover that they weren't for me. I signed my first professional basketball contract for a team in New Castle, Delaware.

The great thing about this pro league in the northeastern United States was that it was a weekend league. I was able to work Monday through Friday and drive just over an hour away for practices and games Friday through Sunday. So what was I to do as I pursued my childhood dream of playing in the NBA and entrepreneurial life?

I still remember sitting on my mom's porch shortly after college graduation.

What am I going to do with my life?

Surely, my predicament is probably familiar to many of you! I was reading *What Color Is Your Parachute?* This book is a great resource that helps people figure out which career path is right for them.

Soon after, I also began my corporate job search. For me, as for many, it seemed like the next logical step after graduating with a business degree.

After trudging through various sales and marketing interviews, the notion that I was born to start something new was affirmed. As far back as I can remember, I was always initiating projects and taking others along for the journey.

Why should now be any different?

As I prayed and thought about what to do with my life, I was challenged to consider that which brings me great joy. At age 21, the three major areas of my life were basketball, inspiring people, and empowering the next generation of kids to move toward their ultimate goals. I saw no reason to wait five minutes, let alone five years to do what I loved. So I decided to combine all three of these elements and start a business! Sounds reasonable, right? While I did have a business education, I had no idea how to begin besides going after the things that made me passionate.

The more I pondered the possibilities, the more passionate I became. I quickly devised a business plan, recruited my older brother, rallied startup money, and hit the ground running. The plan was to use basketball as a vehicle to instill and reinforce life-changing values into children between 5 and 14 through motivational basketball camps, clinics, leagues, instructional coaching, and speaking. Our business grew quickly, and within a few years, we were working with more than 500 kids through our programs each year. Thanks to our early success, we also purchased a basketball clothing brand and formed a performance apparel company.

By the age of 23, I had two businesses and was pursuing an NBA career. After earning a spot on a prestigious summer league all-star team, interest was sparked with the Philadelphia 76ers and the Orlando Magic, but it never panned out. I was thrilled just to have the opportunity!

Then, I met who is now my beautiful wife. I felt compelled to hang up the high tops and refocus my efforts toward starting a family and running more efficient businesses.

I am eternally grateful for my entrepreneurial journey, which has led me to found or co-found 9 different businesses over the past 22 years. Karen and I have now been married for more than 15 years and have three amazing kids, RJ (10), Kayla (8), and Zach (3), and live in West Chester, Pennsylvania. I am the founder of Holman International, a global consultancy that empowers leaders from the inside out through keynote talks, interactive workshops, and books like *Lead the Way* and *All In*. In addition, I am the founder of Meeting House Ministries, a global equipping network helping leaders embrace simple community life.

Teams who share personal stories are more effective.

I love what Francesca Gino, behavioral scientist and Tandon Family Professor of Business Administration at Harvard had to say in her Harvard Business Review article, *Teams Who Share Personal Stories Are More Effective:*

"Research has shown that teams are biased toward repeating information rather than adding new information to the discussion. Why? Because repetition helps members appear competent.

Robin Ely of Harvard Business School and David Thomas, the current dean of Georgetown University's McDonough School of Business, found in a qualitative study of diverse teams that openly discussing the unique qualities of different team members and integrating diverse perspectives allowed individuals to feel valued and respected."

Francesca's article highlights the best way to help team members connect: embracing the story. The more teams are willing to share their unique story, the more valued they will feel. This *inside out* approach will lock in trust and ultimately enhance team performance.

Storytelling connects us in more ways than we know.

Most people want to believe that they are a part of something larger than themselves. When we share personal stories, there is an exchange of life. Although each story is distinct, there is a shared bond that knits us together for the common good. This is what makes us human. When we begin to perceive our humanity together, we share a deeper and greater *connectedness*.

When we embrace this connectedness, life becomes more about people than things. We look after the interests of others in non-manipulative ways. This is authentic connection - the place where you become an integral part of a much broader story than your own. Trust is fortified through healthy lines of communication.

A great resource is Donald Miller's *Building a Story Brand* book. Don is an author, public speaker, business owner, and CEO of StoryBrand, a company that helps businesses clarify their message.

The power of story has everything to do with your willingness to invite team members into your world and encourage them to do the same. When you are dedicated to this intentional practice of connection, trust blooms from the inside out. An authentic anchor of trust has more to do with who a team member is rather than the work they have done. Teams like this cultivate unity through diversity.

Reflection Exercise

Look at your life as a story. Begin to fill in the major components of your personal story. A compelling story can be shared with as much detail or brevity as needed.

Title of your story_____

Situation or desire_____

Complication or obstacle_____

Solution or outcome_____

PART II

Unity in Diversity

CHAPTER 4
Team Dynamics for a Dynamic Team

"Strength lies in differences, not in similarities." - Stephen R. Covey

ARE YOU FAMILIAR WITH ANY of these statements?

"No one does it like I do."

"If they can't do it the right way, I guess I'll just do it myself."

"If only there were two of me right now, everything would be fine."

For many, these sentiments hit way too close to home.

If we're not careful, we can easily fall into the trap of surrounding ourselves with people that heavily validate *our* way. Before we know it, we're spending all of our time with people who look like us, sound like us, think like us, and act like us. And yet, team creativity and completeness is achieved through a diversity of thought.

Do you unload your glasses bottom down or bottom up?

When my wife and I first got married, I used to unload the glasses from the dishwasher to the cabinets right side up. She would place them upside down. I would place a new roll of toilet paper to be pulled from the top, and she would place it to be pulled from the bottom. Of course, I was convinced in both scenarios that my way was right, and hers was wrong!

We had to stop pointing fingers and start honoring the other's perspective. **When you honor the other's perspective, you honor the other person.**

Easier said than done, right?

As I talked about in Chapter 1, Karen and I realized we were choosing stubbornness over presence. This caused some of our disunity and yielded to an *outside in* approach that made us want to change the other.

Coming out of this healing process, we became aware of specific factors that helped us build trust. I call them "team dynamics for a dynamic team."

One of the things we intentionally practiced was sharing *why* we do things the way we do. Subsequently, we discovered some amazing things about each other.

We recognized the need for the other's unique perspective, creative thought, sensitive counsel, practical wisdom, and significant life experience to live to our fullest potential. This realization unveiled the fact that we were *truly* better together. We were spot on!

More than 15 years later, I joke with people - at least, they think I'm joking - that if it weren't for my wife, I would be sucking my thumb and wandering around in the middle of nowhere.

Leadership teams and business relationships are similar to marital relationships, whether in health or dysfunction. If you deeply desire a well-functioning team, be intentional. Find out *why* team members do what they do before you judge.

Who knows, you might actually learn something that catapults your team in a whole new direction!

Peacemaking Creates Unity in Diversity

A few years ago, some tension arose in our local church community. A married couple who was expecting their first child felt a strong urge to serve others in a different country. If taken, this trip would last for an indefinite amount of time.

The parents of the wife really didn't want to see them go. You can't blame them, right? From their perspective, they would miss their daughter, son-in-law, and certainly the birth of their first grandchild. They'd possibly miss the early stages of the baby's development. Different personalities, life stages, and opinions on the same situation left the couple in a difficult spot.

I knew all of the individuals involved and cared deeply for them. So I gathered everyone together and facilitated a discussion within our spiritual community. It was a healthy conversation full of encouragement, understanding, and practical guidance. It was truly one of the most life-giving conversations I've ever witnessed. There was love, honor, and greater understanding of where everyone was coming from. That doesn't mean that there weren't times of disagreement, passion, and even misunderstanding. But there was a willingness and a commitment to work through the discord in a safe community space.

As the meeting concluded and issues had been sifted through, the couple felt an even stronger pull to make the move. Well don't you know, the fruits of their labor were amazing. It turned out to be a one-year trip, during which their little boy was born abroad and received dual citizenship. They received practical help from many friends and family members and faithfully served those in need overseas. The wife's family back home grew in patience, learned to trust God, and built deeper relationships with their children.

The Path of Least Resistance

If we're not careful, we can look up one day and find ourselves surrounded by what I call mini-mes: Individuals and groups who share similar interests, passions, educational backgrounds, life experiences, and values. These people justify our opinions and thought processes. We can't help but subconsciously gravitate toward those that are just like us.

Even if we take steps toward diversity, many of us quickly try to influence our new team members to become more like us anyway!

Why is that? It's comfortable. Who doesn't like feeling validated? It may feel easier, but in truth, a lack of diversity is not nearly as vibrant or fruitful in the long run.

In her 2018 *Houston Chronicle* article, *Advantages and Disadvantages of Diversity in the Workplace*, Linda Emma lists research-based advantages and disadvantages of diversity:

> "*Advantage: Better Financial Results*
> *Advantage: Global-Level Competition*
> *Advantage: Fact-Based Decision-Making*
> *Advantage: Creative and Innovative Thinking*

Advantage: Cross-Cultural Understanding
Disadvantage: Difficulty in Transitioning
Disadvantage: Short-Term Cost Outlay

Just as the Americans with Disabilities Act brought significant changes to some businesses at a financial cost, so will diversity require some flexibility. As employees become more diverse, you may face associated costs that you hadn't considered."

Some of you may be thinking, "This is a lot of work! Is it really worth it?" Well, if global, gender, ethnic, and cultural diversity isn't enough, Steve Forbes provides an additional layer of diversity that is crucial.

My Lunch with Steve Forbes

In 2018 I was honored to meet Steve Forbes, Editor in Chief of Forbes Media, for a two-hour lunch in New York City. During our meeting, Steve openly discussed his family life, positive influences, leadership, team dynamics, technology, money, the current political climate, his two presidential runs, and what he does for fun. Trust me, I was soaking in all the knowledge I could!

Throughout our highly interactive talk, I openly discussed my family, faith, international philanthropy work, keynote speaking, Inside Out Leadership philosophy, *Lead the Way*, aspects of *All In*, and what he thinks about the millennial generation.

One of the most intriguing parts of our conversation was when I asked, "What key attribute gives way to great team dynamics?"

Steve responded, ***"Diversity of thought is invaluable. You need people that think differently in order for the team to maximize its effectiveness."***

Two central qualities that stood out about Steve were his genuine humility and courageous spirit. In the end, a new friendship was born, and we each left feeling inspired about life and leadership.

So with all the challenges of upholding global, gender, ethnic, cultural, and thought diversity, who's still all in?!

Before you get completely overwhelmed, there is good news:

Instead of conflict, you have complement.

It seems much easier to surround yourself with mini-mes, but then how would you grow? Where would the adventure be? If we want to excel in being our full selves, growing, enhancing, and seeing movement and momentum in our businesses and on our teams, it requires a diverse team.

You have one body, many parts. Some people are going to be the feet. Some people are going to be the ears. Some people might take a bit more initiative in the mind. Regardless, all parts are necessary.

Teams not only need a conceptual appreciation and embracing of diversity, but an experiential one.

Again, because we're naturally driven to associate with similar people, teams must take deliberate action to maximize diversity.

Living a purposeful life of diversity helps us appreciate the differences in our team members. It's realizing the value they have. Now that's team dynamics for a dynamic team!

Each member of a team must be the healthiest version of themselves, offering unique perspectives on situations, people, challenges, and opportunities. This collaborative effort amplifies trust.

Three great resources to help bring awareness to diversity are the DISC profile, Myers Briggs, and Strengths Finder 2.0.

In addition, as I mentioned back in Chapter 2, Holman International offers a practical tool called *Discover Your Life Purpose*. This resource helps you assess 5 key areas of your life to better embrace who you are and answer your personal *why*. Imagine if each of your team members took this assessment and convened for an interactive discussion. This assessment tool can be found in a couple of my online courses at: www.InsideOutLeadershipAcademy.com.

Reflection

Read a book in the next 30 days that is not your typical reading material. This will introduce you to new ideas and experiences that are not on your radar. Find something from an author with whom you might disagree. Go into the reading with a friendly heart and a curious mind to see what you can learn from the author.

CHAPTER 5
Developing a Culture of Honor

"Humility forms the basis of honor, just as the low ground forms the foundation of a high elevation." - Bruce Lee

ONE OF THE TEAM DYNAMICS for a dynamic team we discussed last chapter deserves more attention - honoring the other's perspective. If you want trust, grasping this idea is a *big* deal.

I have never been to a memorial service where people spoke poorly about a person - no matter how many bad things he or she did while living. It made me wonder what would happen if we honored people consistently in the workplace in the same way we would at their memorial services.

Usually, there are beautiful songs, powerful testimonies, and encouraging teachings to honor the life of the deceased person. Why can it be so difficult to focus on these things when people are still alive?

As we look for ways to honor people, it launches them into fulfilling their life purpose. The result is a happier work environment and superior performance. As we honor people, we bring honor to ourselves. Remember the simple saying, "Treat others how you would want to be treated."

Regardless of poor choices, annoying habits, obnoxious behaviors, and dysfunctional family backgrounds, each person has been created with the DNA of goodness and a unique destiny to fulfill. What a joy it is to pull the best out of people even when they don't see it in themselves!

To the Degree You Honor Others, You Honor Yourself

Living a life of honor comes most naturally when I really believe that I am uniquely and beautifully created with my own purpose. We tend to project how we view ourselves onto others. So in essence, the more we value and honor ourselves, the more we value and honor others. The mirror of the self and others is how *inside out* teams work.

You've probably heard the saying, "You can only give what you got!" Well, another interesting way to put it is: The amount of honor we give to others is a direct indication of the amount we allow ourselves.

Honor Knows No Bounds

Years ago, I started a non-profit organization. It was an exciting time as our community reach grew substantially, both locally and globally. Our core leadership team consisted of a handful of volunteers, some full-time staff, and some part-time staff. There was no better time for someone like me, who likes to work myself out of a job, to transition into a new venture.

After just 5 short years, my building process came to an end. Those that know me know that I only start new things if I can quickly find people who are far more intelligent, gifted, and skilled at taking it to a whole new level.

In preparation for this new chapter in our lives, my local church had a special service to bless my wife and I with words of encouragement and prayer. Little did I know, they had created a special video of encouraging words, stories, and biblical references about our life. To put it mildly, I was blown away!

I was completely surprised as tears of joy and love filled my heart. I was forever changed. I experienced genuine appreciation and respect in a way that is difficult to describe. **This is the power of honor.**

This profound act of kindness gave me a confidence that energized my new venture. I felt like people were there for me, and so I could accomplish anything. I watched that video off and on for the first two years as I built the new organization. It provided a much-needed dose of encouragement to weather the storms of transition.

As you probably guessed, a culture of honor is a key ingredient when building team trust. As you feel inclined to do so, look for opportunities to surprise team members with intentional ways to honor them.

Of course, it is easier to honor those that deserve it. Nevertheless, there will be times when you are challenged to honor those that hurt you.

Sometimes honor is giving people what they don't deserve.

Many people give others what they deserve. This is especially the case when someone is stripped of their title or position due to bad behavior. If someone treats you kindly, your natural instinct is to return the kindness. If someone is nasty, it's easy to rationalize being nasty right back, isn't it? If someone hits you hard, it's ok to seek revenge, right? If a team member doesn't follow through with a deadline, we often jump to reprimanding them, either mentally or out loud.

"What a lousy job they did!"

We have grown so accustomed to this "tit for tat" way of living and leading. Sure, there can be a sense of instant gratification or even some short-term gain. But does it yield long-term vibrancy in the relationship? Just because something feels normal and the vast majority conform to it doesn't make it right.

Some might be thinking, "Come on, Robb! Are you one of those guys who let's team members get away with whatever they want? That is soft leadership. What we need is to hold people accountable."

Please know that I'm not saying there aren't times when we should give people what they deserve for a greater good. But there is something to be said for a leadership style that honors people when they least expect it.

I've learned that the secret of honor is to give people what they don't deserve. When we do, they are caught off guard in a really good way. It interrupts the norm for all the right reasons.

This truth was clearly revealed to me while out at a restaurant with some friends. Our waiter was awful. If there was any little thing that could go wrong during the meal, it did! The service was poor, the waiter's attitude was undesirable, and the food was subpar. When you spend good money, it's only fitting to get what you pay for, right?

As frustration mounted, the meal came to a close. Strangely, I felt a little nudge inside of me to give the waiter twice as much as I would to someone who did a great job.

No, that can't be right.

I brushed off the thought. But the feeling grew stronger and the idea louder from the deepest place in my heart. Against every fiber of my being, I left a tip that I had never left before.

I wasn't there to see the waiter's reaction, but I have faith that it changed the course of his day - maybe even his life!

Departing from the restaurant that day, I learned the following:

- We should never assume we know exactly why someone does or doesn't do something.
- If we always give people what they deserve, they will likely never reach the fullness of who they were created to be!
- Could it be that when we give people what they don't deserve, it's a prime opportunity to reach them from the inside out? Quite possibly, we can reach them in a place they would never be reached otherwise.

I visited another restaurant with two friends a couple years ago to catch up and discuss our careers. Shortly after being seated, we were approached by a very friendly waitress. She asked us our names and what we wanted to drink. We responded by asking her what her name was and sparked some brief, yet friendly conversation. During our two-hour meal, time flew by. Isn't that how it always is with people you enjoy?

I told my friends I wanted to treat them to the meal. They declined at first, but eventually, they graciously accepted. As I was paying for the meal, I wanted to honor this young woman's socks off! I decided to go above and beyond what even *she* deserved - and she deserved a great tip for her demeanor, positivity, kindness, and service.

As we were about to leave, she came running out from the kitchen with tears in her eyes. She gave me a big hug and expressed how much the tip meant to her. As it turns out, she and her grandmother had been struggling financially and living in a car not long before that. The act of honor spoke to her. It told her she would be taken care of, and that her life had meaning. This one simple act of kindness demonstrated honor for a total stranger, infusing meaning, purpose, and significance into our exchange.

I don't know what it is with me and restaurants, but wherever a lesson is learned, we can apply it in every little area of our lives. As it relates to forging trust within teams, **it is always useful to see things in others that they might not see in themselves.** Honor is one way to accomplish just that.

Sometimes bestowing honor is giving people who do the least the greatest reward. At other times, it's giving people who do the best even greater rewards.

Give Based On Honor, Not Just Need

It doesn't take long to see the needs that exist all around us. Whether it be among our families, friends, neighbors, and even our team members. The larger the need, the more it reveals an obvious opportunity to serve that team member. Typically, we serve by meeting a need through intentional time, resources, and/or expended energy.

But what about when there is not an obvious need?

A good friend once shared with me, *"We should give based on honor, not just need."*

I learned this valuable lesson years ago when my good friend reached out to a number of his friends to invite them into a financial partnership for his upcoming humanitarian trip. It's important to note that he had the means to fund the entire trip himself.

To his total surprise, not many friends took him up on the offer. This left him discouraged and wondering how such a thing could happen in his close circle of friends. The problem was that many of these people knew he had the financial means to meet his own needs. Thus they didn't respond to the amazing opportunity.

When we give to people based on who they are, not merely because they need something, it fuels a culture of honor. This *inside out* way of living with our team members builds trust simply by holding them in high regard.

One Body, Many Parts

A true team is made up of one body with many parts. No position, title, or responsibility is more valuable than the rest. When we believe this, we are free to honor each team member equally.

Sadly, our American culture places certain titles, degrees, and positions above others in a hierarchy. But when we learn that true leadership is service, every member of the team or organization can shine as one body of unified parts working together.

Who has better modeled this idea than basketball coach Phil Jackson of the 1996 Chicago Bulls? (Go figure, I'm working in another sports illustration!) Phil had big talent and even bigger egos to manage. This was the year the Bulls arguably had one of the best seasons in basketball history with a 72-10 record and a championship win against the Seattle Supersonics.

They had the most coveted player in the league, Michael Jordan, the best complimentary player, Scottie Pippen, and the best defense player, Dennis Rodman. How was Phil Jackson to coach such egos and such talent, along with all of the other players on the team, like sharp shooter Steve Kerr?

He pulled it off by showing each player that they were just as important and valuable as the next, from top dog Michael Jordan to the last practice player. If they were going to win, Phil knew it would be because each player believed in that philosophy.

Another great example is NBA Hall of Famer, Bill Russell. Bill holds the record for the most NBA championships won with 11 titles during his 13-year playing career. He won his first championship with the Boston Celtics in his rookie year. He then went on to win 10 championships in the next 12 years, including 8 consecutive championships from 1959-1966. He won his last 2 championships in 1968 and 1969 as a coach.

One of the things that made Bill so special was his understanding of honor. He knew that if his team was truly going to excel, they would need to demonstrate honor and make personal sacrifices for the betterment of the team.

Take-Aways from the Basketball Court

If we want to develop a culture of honor, we must know:

1. No team member is any more valuable than another.
2. Each team member must feel a genuine sense of appreciation.
3. The leader/coach sets the tone through words and actions.
4. Team members make personal sacrifices for the betterment of the whole.

Keep the bar low and you'll be pleasantly surprised.

I've found that placing very low expectations on people in my life goes a long way. When people first hear that, they can't help but go, "Really? But expectations are important!"

Yes, expectations can be a good thing, but many of us go through life with unhealthy expectations. This perpetuates frustration and discourages us more than we'd like to admit. Sounds like an *outside in* approach, doesn't it?

With an *inside out* approach, we remember that people are people. Things happen. We also realize that when someone truly values something, they will go out of their way to be present - even giving you the shirt off their back if needed. Staying consistently connected to your team members is a critical part of the process.

Not long ago, I noticed that one of my team members was increasingly checking out of our workplace culture. We would also get together one-on-one, but that connection was also dissipating. To his credit, he had a lot going on: a new marriage, new career position, and many other things tugging on him. It all required some adjustment. Being attuned to this, I simply extended grace and accepted where he was at in life. I knew the season would eventually come to an end.

During this time of adjustment, I kept the bar really low for him. I didn't expect him to be as involved as he once was. **This decision freed me to honor him more for who he was than for his contribution**.

A lot of time passed, and we didn't meet to catch up or clear the air, which fueled some small misunderstandings. But eventually we were able to reunite and be fully present with one another. As a result of our efforts, the friendship grew, and our bond became stronger than ever.

Honor is recognizing that people are more important than what they do or don't do for you and your team. Lowering the bar and releasing our unhealthy expectations helps others feel honored.

One Practical Way to Help You Keep Your Honor

Team members need to know that you personally care. Good organizations have a professional development track for their people. Great organizations have a personal development track that feeds into a professional track for their people.

If we want to maximize the potential of each team member, getting to know them as human beings more than human doings is key. What would it look like to spend a little time each month with each of your core team members? How could you get to know them a little better?

At the end of the day, it's all about trust. Here is one simple way to help build and foster trust through genuine relationship:

Devote time monthly with each of your team members. There will be some temptation to discuss work-related issues. Resist the urge and spend time talking about life, what interests them, what are they passionate about, etc. Each time you meet with them, make it your mission to find out something new about them and share something new about you.

In summary, I have learned that developing a culture of honor has everything to do with honoring yourself first. This is *inside out* leadership at its best. When we hold ourselves in high regard (by embracing who we are), we are compelled to honor others. From here, we have a wealth of opportunity to celebrate our team members and honor their socks off!

As we spend more intentional time with team members, we will learn to identify a need and honor them in meeting it. And if we can honor them without any need, even better!

One more thing: Always create space to put the personal before the professional. Personal connection is imperative not only for maintaining trust, but for moving through inevitable conflicts with grace (more about this in the next chapter).

Reflection:

1. What are three specific things you honor about yourself?
2. Who is one team member you can intentionally connect with and honor in the next 30 days? What is a creative way to honor them?
3. During your next team meeting, facilitate a time of honor. Go around the room to each team member and encourage all to share specific things they like about them as people and professionals.

CHAPTER 6
Turning Conflict into a Creative Superpower

"Every person in this life has something to teach me, and as soon as I accept that, I open myself to truly listening." -
Catherine Doucette

THE AVERAGE HUMAN BEING AND professional dislikes conflict. Mainly, this is because people find it much easier (at least in the short term) to avoid confrontation even when they know it's inevitable.

Let's say someone musters up the strength and courage to confront another person. How they go about it usually sets them up for a volatile interaction, which only escalates the conflict. If there is one thing I think kids growing up in the education system should learn more, it's healthy conflict resolution. Unfortunately, it's just not taught enough. This puts people, including leaders, in a trial and error learning process. **Thus most people engage with conflict in 1 of 3 ways: passive aggression, anger, or suppression.**

All three approaches result in a narrative much like my early marriage story in Chapter 1. When we react in any of these 3 ways, it's an *outside in* approach. We're attempting to change our team members to meet our needs instead of changing ourselves to meet their needs.

Thankfully, there is a better way!

We must work through our insecurities from the inside out. To do this, we need to understand how our brains work so we can use them for a greater good.

In his Psychology Today article, *Under Pressure: Your Brain on Conflict*, Ph.D. Joshua Gowin provides a glimpse into how the human brain functions:

"The hippocampus, the brain region responsible for forming new <u>memories</u>, is particularly sensitive to cortisol. When released after an emotionally charged experience, cortisol can sear memories into our brain; it tells our brain the message was important.

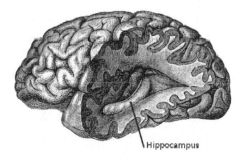

Hippocampus

But like the boy who cried wolf, too much of a strong signal can have a numbing effect. Over time, stress-induced cortisol release, if at continually high levels, might damage your hippocampus.

The best-protected individuals buoy themselves with strong social support networks. They turn to friends and family, which helps stabilize cortisol levels. Conflict can make us feel that our position within a group is in jeopardy; this potential exclusion may be the most painful part of losing. Your loved ones may offer solutions to your problem, but more importantly, they confirm your status."

I love the fact that Gowin highlights the need for strong social support networks. You need a community you can turn to in order to resolve conflicts in a healthy way. If not, you're headed down a path of isolation.

Community Is Crucial

I was facilitating an interactive training on conflict resolution when an image about isolation and community popped into my head. Over the years, I've grown more confident in expressing the images that flash into my mind during keynote talks or interactive training sessions. It's so much fun!

Here's the image: Imagine two boxers in a ring. One is you, and the other is your opponent. But the opponent is not the other person with whom you are in conflict. It's a destructive force looking to destroy your relationship. When you are tired, stressed, and anxious over a conflict, it's as though this destructive force has you cornered in the ring. It delivers a crushing blow that leaves you helpless on the ground. As it towers over you in your loneliness, it seems as though you've been defeated. This is the imprisonment that isolation can bring during a conflict.

In steps community.

When you have a life-giving community of people in your corner, they help you know who you're truly up against—Remember, it's not who you think —and how to pick your battles. When you find yourself cornered in the ring, your community acts as your trainer saying, "Get up! You can do this!"

If you've done a good job growing a diverse organization with different viewpoints, healthy conflict resolution skills are essential for developing *inside out* leaders and trusting teams.

It's time to turn conflict into a creative superpower! But before we do, it's important to understand the seasons of a team and the effects it can have on conflict.

Psychologist Bruce Tuckman first came up with the memorable phrase "Forming, Storming, Norming, and Performing" in his 1965 article, *Developmental Sequence in Small Groups*.

In the **forming** stage, teams are just getting to know one another. There may be both excitement and anxiety as roles have not yet been established. This is when strong leadership and guidance is most needed.

In the **storming** stage, things get shaken up. This is when conflict may first arise as team members get comfortable in their roles and begin to assert themselves. If major problems are not worked through, teams don't make it past this stage. Incompatibilities come to the surface here.

In the **norming** stage, conflict resolution takes place as team bonds strengthen and deepen. Ideally, team members recognize each others strengths, respect their leaders, and even socialize well together. Significant productivity and growth often occurs here.

In the **performing** stage, a team can begin to reach its initial goals. The structures put forth by leadership allow work to flow smoothly and predictably. Leaders can delegate tasks and focus on the growth of each team member.

Now that we understand the seasons of organizational development, let's tackle conflict. Healthy conflict resolution has three aspects:

1. Self-assertion
2. Active listening
3. Collaboration

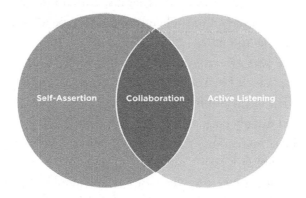

Assuming you are building trust and deepening your connections with a diverse team, things aren't always picture perfect. At the end of the day, we're human. Diversity will bring differences that can rub team members the wrong way.

We are not looking for a perfect team, but one that is committed to an *inside out* process that fosters trust.

In which season of development do you think the most conflict arises? You guessed it - the *storming season*!

As we know, conflict can pop up at any time, but it's helpful to foresee the tumultuous periods so we can prepare accordingly. I don't know about you, but I don't like being caught off guard about anything, conflicts especially.

Remember when we talked about proactive communication back in Chapter 2? It's always better to be proactive than reactive, especially when a conflict is on the table.

How to Handle Healthy Conflict Resolution

All conflicts involve at least two parties. Typically, there is a team member who initiates the conversation and one who is the recipient.

Let's say a team member did something, knowingly or unknowingly, that rubbed you the wrong way. Whether it was an hour ago, a day ago, or even a year ago, you feel an unspoken tension. Maybe it has even become the 'elephant in the room.'

Every time you are around that person or hear their name, that tension rises up a little bit. You know you should say something, but you don't know what to say or how they will react.

Maybe you usually back off and hope that time will heal all wounds, but the strain is increasing. You've finally reached your tipping point. Enough is enough!

So you initiate a meeting with your team member because you are committed to living and leading from the inside out.

Self-assertion is the first basic communication skill that helps turn conflict into a creative superpower. This includes expressing concerns strategically in ways that minimize defensiveness.

Self-assertion honors your integrity and worth.

Conflict has the potential to create heightened emotions and stress. Self-assertion is not just for the team member initiating the conversation, but for any team member who is verbally involved at any time during the meeting.

Some advantages of self-assertion:

- Generates mutual respect and trust
- Facilitates collaboration
- Useful for high priority conflicts when the relationship is important

Some disadvantages:

- Takes time
- Requires risk and vulnerability
- Requires skill

Self-assertion has four key elements.

First, you must paint a picture of what took place at the time of the conflict. This is called **concrete data**. In other words, it's the simple, agreed-upon, neutral facts that keep both team members on the same page. Think about it: You are beginning your meeting with factual, observable data. You can't go wrong with that!

Second, share your **feelings**. Once the facts are presented, it's time to share your subjective experience. It helps the other person understand the significance of your concern. When you express your personal feelings, the use of non-accusatory words is invaluable. Stay away from phrases like *you always, you did,* and, *you never.*

Swap those out for "When _____ (concrete data), I felt _____ (your subjective experience).

In addition, steer clear of beginning a question with "why."

Why did you say that? Why did you do that? It instantly makes the person on the receiving end feel like they did something wrong. When we use choice words (I call them cushion words), it keeps our defenses low and allows both people to stay honored in a safe environment.

You may say something like, *"I don't understand what you were thinking when you made that statement. Can you explain a little more?"* That feels different than, *"Why did you say that?"* Something as subtle as changing one word in the beginning of a question can have a huge impact.

Third, it is necessary to share the **consequences** - the impact the issue had on you. Ask yourself why you think there is a problem. If you just share your feelings without explaining the reasoning behind them, your team member will only receive half the message. We want them in on all of it!

Fourth, the **tone of inquiry** communicates openness to hearing the other's view. This sets you up for a one-to-one chat instead of playing the blame game.

A formula for self-assertion (past):

When (concrete data) _____, I felt _____, because _____ (consequences).

A formula for self-assertion (future):

If (concrete action) _____, I would feel _____, because _____ (consequences).

Active listening is the second basic communication skill that will turn conflict into a creative superpower. This includes reflecting what the person is saying, inquiring with direct questions, summarizing, and testing what you've heard. You want to clarify the meaning of what the other person is saying.

Whereas self-assertion honors your worth, active listening honors your team member's worth.

Let's face it, the average leader, team member, and human being does not excel at active listening. As discussed back in Chapter 1, these learned behaviors begin at a very young age.

I'm reminded of a time in kindergarten when my teacher gave clear instructions to space out our floor mats for rest time. I didn't listen to what she said - or maybe I did but chose not to obey - and shimmied over to the closest classmate. I then proceeded to talk to her until I got caught. It was all about what *I* wanted to do, not what was best for my classmates. Needless to say, 5-year-old me learned a hard lesson that day.

Sadly, we see this same pattern play out in adults in various social spheres. A lack of active listening skills causes those around us to shut down. They don't feel valued or appreciated.

What are the topics we are told to stay away from at big family celebrations? You guessed it: politics, religion, and money!

I think it's because people are so passionate about getting their response in that they don't hear or understand what the other person is really saying. Let's cut to the chase: We are not skilled listeners because we want to prove that we are right and others are wrong.

It is more important to love than to be right.

I'm not saying that we shouldn't communicate our feelings and confront people when necessary. But *how* we do it is the difference between conflict and collaboration.

An active listener withholds immediate counterarguments and doesn't re-assert their viewpoint right away. This frees them to:

- Acknowledge what is being said
- Test the meaning behind the other person's words
- Encourage the other person to elaborate
- Actively explore their own perspective

It is a great way to remain curious, fully understand, and appreciate another person's ideas.

One practical way to use active listening is to **reflect** back what the person is saying. Don't worry, you don't have to interrupt them constantly. Wait a bit to gather some data and feeling. Then repeat back the essential meaning of what they said. Trust is solidified when we allow others to feel heard.

Another practical tool is **inquiry**. Asking open-ended questions while keeping your personal assumptions and interpretations in check is key here.

Lastly, I've found that **summarizing** what you believe the other is saying is a great way to master active listening. This takes concerted focus and energy until you get the hang of it. It's kind of like learning to walk for the first time.

It can be as simple as, "I am hearing you say_____ (summarize). Is that correct?"

Collaboration is the third basic communication skill that will turn conflict into a creative superpower. It involves mutual understanding and joint problem-solving.

Healthy conflict resolution should always lead to **collaboration**. Self-assertion honors my integrity and worth, active listening honors my team member's integrity and worth, and collaboration honors both. Self-assertion and active listening allow for **mutual benefit**.

In collaborative problem-solving, team members find common ground so they don't have to repeat the same unhealthy cycle in the future.

A couple of strategies you may want to use for joint problem-solving are:

- Come up with a few basic things you are both willing to agree on to ensure healthier communication moving forward (e.g. meet more frequently to get on the same page, commit to practicing this process with someone else in your life, etc.)
- Discuss some ground rules if a future conflict were to arise (e.g. agree on a similar process as this to work through, etc.)

I will never forget what my late business mentor, Lee Farmelo - who taught me most of what I know about healthy conflict resolution - said to me about this process: *"There is only one way to get better at it—practice!"* I still remember my first homework assignment: Go home and talk to my wife about a recent conflict, going through the steps with her. I did it with some fear and hesitation. But ultimately we found value in it, and our communication grew stronger than ever.

In summary, it doesn't take long for a leader to discover that people are multifaceted. We come from different backgrounds, have different personalities, and express different worldviews. When tension escalates, we can be reactive, resulting in an *outside in* approach that feeds passive aggression, anger, or suppression. Or we can choose to be proactive, resulting in an *inside out* approach that embraces healthy conflict resolution and honors you and your team member's integrity.

Now it's your turn to be All In.

Reflection

Role-playing is essential in helping team members get better at these skills. Select a recent conflict you had with a friend or spouse. Take the initiative and lead them through the process of self-assertion, active listening, and collaboration. What was your overall result? What was your greatest strength? Greatest weakness? Lessons learned?

Are you now ready to take this initiative in the workplace?

PART III
Power in Shared Vision

CHAPTER 7
Igniting Team Empowerment

"As we look ahead into the next century, leaders will be those who empower others." - Bill Gates

ALL IN REQUIRES A DEPTH of commitment.

As we have learned, when team members are deeply committed to connection and unity, trust is built from the inside out. This foundation becomes the anchor for a **shared vision**.

How teams share their vision has changed dramatically over the years. In the past, the charismatic leader would use their personality, charm, and passion to call people to action.

Come on! Who's climbing the mountain with me?

It's a different day and age, and companies are learning that everyone's voice matters. We're shifting away from the "do it because I said so" mentality and tapping into the wisdom in the room.

When everyone gets to contribute in the creative process, teams as a whole find greater empowerment. We don't necessarily find empowerment by crafting a vision statement and reciting it. Teams need values that they are committed to living together.

Peter Demarest is the author of *Answering the Central Question* and a thought leader in integrating axiology (the study of value) and neuroscience. He writes:

"Success in life, love, and leadership requires making good value judgments. Real personal power is in knowing which choices and actions will create the greatest net value. It's about getting very clear about what you really value, making good choices, and then taking appropriate actions. When you are value-centric, it's not all about you; it's about adding value, period. Your intention is to create the greatest possible net value for everyone, including yourself. The value-centric person thinks in terms of The Central Question: What choice can I make and action can I take, in this moment, to create the greatest net value?"

We Value What We Do

So often people *aspire* to a set of core values. In reality, core values are what we already do.

When we begin to identify the values we are already living, we can make a clear distinction between those values and the values we aspire to live.

Years ago, my business hosted a leadership seminar to inspire people in their personal purpose and shared vision. I gave the keynote address, and afterwards, some leaders approached me to tell me how much it impacted them. I must say, I am always humbled and honored by such feedback.

As the crowd dispersed, I was approached by a particular individual who sparked something in me. This guy was upbeat and hungry – a real learner. As we talked, I quietly thought, "Man, this is a guy I would like to get to know!

"Can we get together and chat more about life and business?" he asked.

Without hesitation, I responded with an emphatic, "YES!"

Now, as a leader, I don't readily agree to many things on the spot. For each yes I give, I'm saying no to a hundred other things. But this was different. I felt it, and I knew this had the potential to become a meaningful friendship.

We started meeting up regularly over a cup of coffee, and it became clear that we were developing a deep friendship. It wasn't because of what he could do for me or what I could do for him. We were simply exchanging life based on mutual respect for one another. This went beyond bonding over some personal interests.

Over time, business opportunities flourished, and the friendship led to deep trust in one another. We teamed up for a podcast before podcasts were even 'mainstream' and sat on the advisory boards for each other's companies.

Years later, this bedrock of trust has helped us push each other to stretch beyond our comfort zone. We gave a voice to our knowledge and experience with an entertaining and therapeutic podcast called White Collar Therapy (www.WhiteCollarTherapy.com). I would never have guessed how much my sphere of influence would grow as a result of one friendship built on trust and shared values.

Here are some of the shared values that continue to empower our team:

Fun: The Lighter Side of Leadership

There's direction, vision, service, strategy, conflict resolution, tasks, putting out fires, mentorship, strategic alliances, training, partnerships, financial projections, problem-solving, team dynamics, and so much more! This is a day in the life of so many influential leaders, and you might have a desire to lighten up! It all sounds so serious and intense. Does it have to be?

There is a lighter side of leadership that is spelled F-U-N! We absolutely must give ourselves permission to enjoy the journey, not take things too seriously (especially ourselves), and have some good 'ol fashion fun!

I'm reminded of a time when I felt guilty doing things inside and outside of work that were fun. In a weird way, I believed that if I had too much fun, it would detract from my focus, goals, and ultimately, my dream. So even if I decided to engage in a fun activity, my mind couldn't shut off from work. Is anyone with me on this one?

In light of this ongoing mental battle, I finally reached a breaking point and said, "Enough is enough. Something has to change!"

This opened up avenues for intentionally having more fun inside and outside of the office - including leadership fun. As a result, my productivity drastically improved along with my team's productivity. Over time, intentional fun became a lifestyle. **Fun shifted from something I did to someone who I was.**

When we are having fun, it breathes life into ordinary situations. We start to see people and things from a totally new lens. Fun creates a looser environment where people are free to be themselves and offer creative solutions to big problems.

A few practical questions to consider:

- Do you have an awareness of *fun*?
- What intentional steps can you take to have more fun inside and outside of work?
- How can fun become more of who you are as opposed to what you do?

A Culture of Celebration

How many team meetings have you been to that were clearly more problem-focused than solution-focused? I've seen many teams get sucked into the drama of what *isn't* being done while ignoring what *is* being done. In time, this pattern takes a toll on the team and damages the organization's culture.

Can you imagine a work environment where celebration was infused into what you do? Imagine your team intentionally looking for the good in every situation regardless of what they are facing. Imagine team meetings becoming opportunities to encourage each other and support the good that is happening. Imagine if sharing inspiring stories in one-on-one and team meetings was the norm. What if your team looked forward to waking up and coming to work?

So do you just stick your head in the sand about the problems, Robb? NO!

It's from this place of celebration that you and your team have the right attitude, posture, heart, and creativity to *solve* problems. Creative problem-solving thrives in a climate of celebration. The best ideas, thoughts, solutions, and inventions exist in celebration mode. You will find that you naturally work from a place of gratitude instead of aspiring toward it.

One practical thing you can do is have your team participate in a 30-day gratitude challenge. All you need is a designated gratitude wall, different color sticky notes (one color per team member), and team members that are All In. As soon as team members arrive at the office, they write 5 things for which they are grateful and place them on the wall. At the end of the month, the whole wall is covered with expressions of gratitude.

This practice can be at the start of the day, before every formal team meeting, or even when a team member hits one of their goals. Remember, a victory for one is a victory for all! Whether your team meets in a physical or virtual space, this celebratory practice can be instilled anywhere.

Serve One Another

Years ago, I heard a teacher say something that has always stuck with me.

"Shepherds always smell like sheep."

Think about it: shepherds lead, feed, guide, correct, and are always there to serve their sheep in any way possible. They are in the trenches with them, getting messy, and yet faithfully serving those in their sphere of influence. This is at the heart of what we discussed back in Chapter 5 on developing a culture of honor.

'Bottom up' leadership looks to elevate those above you. In other words, instead of looking to get noticed, you notice others first. It's an act of genuine humility.

When in a position of leadership, we are often tempted to think that we are better than others. Maybe we consciously or subconsciously think, "I'm too good for that," or "That's for them, not me!" This is quite dangerous as it slowly erects a barrier between ourselves and everyone else.

On the other hand, think of a workplace where team members mutually submit to and serve one another. Wow!

Now, this can unfold in one of two ways: You can do it to gain something, or you can do it with no strings attached.

One of the most powerful and practical ways to serve your team is through the art of coaching.

A Coaching Style of Leadership

A key element in leadership and team development is coaching. Coaches can accelerate leadership development by providing guidance and helping aspiring leaders develop their own skill sets. Unfortunately, some people must learn to accept that they need such guidance or it's simply not available to them. If you assume you already know everything, you will miss all your chances to learn and grow.

Teaching your next generation of leaders to see the value in coaching and equipping them with the tools to seek out coaches they need will empower them to reach out sooner.

I find that the most gifted coaches often know the answer, but they ask the critical questions that bring about an epiphany in their client. This way, the client can figure things out for themselves. It teaches them a new way to discover their own insights through questioning.

Coaches serve by coming along for the ride. They are **committed to serving by asking the right questions.** By doing this, clients can hear themselves talk. The discussion may include a lot of what they already knew, but maybe they've never been able to express their insights verbally. So they get it out, and they start exploring. As they share their heart and mind, they begin to have 'aha moments.'

A lot of people get involved in other people's lives and come up with solutions *for* them, but then *they're* responsible for the other person's problems. Aha moments allow for true self-empowerment. The coach isn't responsible for your problems - you are! The coach just holds you accountable for solving them. That's the big difference between coaching and other forms of mentoring.

Here are some practical coaching questions you can ask:

What's standing in your way?
Can you tell me more?
What will happen If you don't take this step?
What does success look like?
What are your 5 whys?
What are you most proud of?
What do you want?
What have you done to try to solve the problem?
What are you doing to *not* achieve your goal?
If your main obstacle didn't exist, how would your life look?
What do you need most right now?

What will things look like after you're successful?

What is the most important thing in the world to you, and why?

What's important about that to you?

So what?

Why not?

Give a man a fish, and he eats for a day. Teach him to fish, and he eats for a lifetime. That pretty much sums it up.

Leaders often feel a strong pull to chime in on someone's life with an answer. You might have history with that same problem, or a poignant experience, etc. But if we can discipline ourselves and hold back from giving answers, we can instead start asking questions. That shift in conversational dynamics is huge. It takes discipline, and it takes intentionality, but it is worth it.

Steve Van Valin, former QVC Culture Catalyst and CEO of Culturology says, *"One of our goals when I was leading the culture at QVC was to **create what we call a coaching rich environment within our culture.** Can you imagine what that would look like where everyone is helping each other out? After a number of years I almost gave up on the idea of teaching people how to coach, because we discovered that it's so much easier for people to ask for coaching.*

If I ask Fred, 'Hey Fred, I'm going to work on this. Will you observe some things from your perspective and see how I could be better?' I've just hired him as my coach. He's free; it's not like I'm paying someone, right? So that gives him permission, through his eyes and ears, to give that coaching to me. We've had a lot higher payoff on that rather than teaching Fred to coach because he'd still have to go through the emotional hurdles to say, 'Jeez, is Steve going to receive this well?'

This could apply to any of us who are trying to work on our practice and profession - Solicit coaching from each other. Beg for it, and be very specific. If you ask, 'How did I do?' and they respond, 'You did great,' that doesn't help. **Give some details and tell them what feedback you're looking for, and they will give you gold in that regard.**"

In addition to asking pivotal questions, good coaches also know the difference between **"911" issues** and general long-term coaching.

Team members may have a bit of an emergency or a pressing matter. It may weigh on them and ultimately hinder their performance. In these instances, I make it a consistent point to ask them: **"What's the number one thing that's keeping you up at night?** This 911 issue will often hang over their head and serve as the subconscious lens through which they see all of their work. This is a great opportunity to serve a team member. Ask this question to aid them in working through more immediate issues.

As important as it is to serve someone with an urgent matter, it is equally important to establish where a team member is and where they want to be. Companies often refer to it as a professional development track. Assisting professionals in working through their priorities, goals, and action steps is long-term coaching.

Reflection

When a team is committed to living a set of values together, it ignites team empowerment. But let's not put the cart before the horse! First, live out your values together. Then, find words that adequately describe that way of being.

Exercise: What are 3-5 values that you and your team members are clearly already living? When you convey these values together, how do they make you and your team feel? Be specific. What is the positive impact these values have on your life and profession? Which values do you feel you can consciously cultivate together?

CHAPTER 8
Team Intuition: Where Breakthroughs Happen

"Intuition is the highest form of intelligence, transcending all individual abilities and skills." - Sylvia Clare

W E IGNITE TEAM EMPOWERMENT BY living our intentional values. And we stoke the fire by understanding and embracing team intuition.

Intuition is *direct knowing* that relies on the non-sequential processing of information. It incorporates both emotions and unconscious thoughts. We are not aware of any reasoning that preceded our solution; the answer appears suddenly and cannot be traced back to anything tangible. Intuition is usually accompanied by a sense of certainty, which makes it distinct from qualified guessing.

Intuition is the acquiring of knowledge and the making of decisions through emotions.

Scientist Bruce Lipton's research shows that the subconscious mind interprets 20,000,000 environmental stimuli per second, while the conscious mind interprets just 40.

Some of the most brilliant minds speak highly of intuition.

Apple CEO Tim Cooke said, *"Intuition is something that occurs in the moment, and if you are open to it, if you listen to it, it has the potential to direct or redirect you in a way that is best for you."*

Albert Einstein spoke openly on the importance of intuition, stating that the rational mind serves the intuition - not the other way around. Coming from a scientist, this may sound surprising. But Einstein believed that intuition was a long-forgotten gift of the human psyche.

Making a Case for Intuition

Let's begin in the head and talk about how most leaders function from there. Most of us are familiar with two of the most common methods of measuring intelligence. One has been around since 1908 - the work of Alfred Binet. It's the IQ (Intelligence Quotient). The other began to surface in 1995 thanks to the work of Daniel Goleman - EQ (Emotional Quotient).

IQ measures cognitive intelligence based on logic and reason, whereas EQ measures personal and social intelligence. Simply put, IQ is often called 'book smarts,' while EQ is more like 'street smarts.'

Experts often insist that if leaders operate in one of these - or better yet, both - they would perform at a much higher level. EQ has been gaining traction in the last few years, clearly distinguishing itself from IQ. But we're also discovering how they work together.

I want to emphasize that there is certainly a time and place for IQ and EQ. However, they both share a common bond: They arise from our conscious thoughts, or the head. Even EQ tends to intellectualize emotion. This can lean toward a more *outside in* approach.

When we navigate from the head to the heart, we find something distinctly unique - our intuition. Much of our intuition lies dormant in the subconscious, a less tangible but more dynamic place from which to live and lead. Some refer to intuition as the "sixth sense," but to demystify it, we can describe it as the place where our life experience shapes our deepest feelings, imagination, and sensitivity at lighting speed. Flashes of insight are usually accompanied by a sense of certainty, which separates them from qualified guessing. It's like the age-old advice, *"Just go with your gut!"*

Think about when a married person shares their relationship story.

"I knew the moment we met that I would spend the rest of my life with him!"

Interesting, right? How did they know? Now you might want to check back with them after a few years to see if that's still true (ha!). However, I think we'd all agree there is something lurking beyond IQ and EQ.

I remember a time in my business when my core team strongly opposed the idea of hiring a new team member. They assumed it might scatter our focus and direct energy away from the company vision. However, I immediately knew I was supposed to hire this person. Even though I had this strong intuition, I still took time to seek counsel and weigh the pros and cons of the decision. As a result, I ended up hiring her. She turned out to be an overwhelmingly positive addition to our team, and funny enough, she enhanced clarity of our vision.

Reflection

Spend 5 minutes recalling some times when you relied on your intuition. What were the results?

Barriers to Intuition

In her 2015 Forbes article, *Intuition Is an Essential Leadership Tool,* Bonnie Marcus talks about the two factors that prevent us from using our intuition: trust and credibility.

1.) "The leaders I interviewed learned to skillfully use and trust their intuition or gut feel. Consistently, they told me that a nagging feeling signaled them to dig into an issue further. Their feeling pointed them to something that needed resolution. The little nagging feeling brings information from your own experience that is stored in less accessible parts of the brain. When we shove away the feeling, we shove away intelligence.

*2.) Intuition definitely has a **credibility problem**. Both men and women expressed an unwillingness to talk about Infotuitive decision-making in a business setting. Instead, several leaders noted that they would find the decision that just felt right and afterwards line up data to support the decision. They needed an understandable way to explain their decision to others. Part of the credibility gap, I believe, can be bridged when we understand the neuroscience behind intuition. It's not woo-woo; it is a practical leadership tool."*

Historically, business leaders have not wanted to discuss, let alone train their teams in intuitive decision-making because it doesn't seem as safe and tangible as using logic or emotional intelligence. But because businesses need quicker and more effective strategic decisions, leaders are increasingly more open to this intangible, yet powerful resource.

CEB's Insight IQ research showed that of 5,000 managers polled, 19% are "visceral decision-makers" who use intuition for nearly all decisions. Journal research shows that intuition plays a key role in decision-making worldwide. For example, research of small and medium-sized enterprises in Africa revealed that intuition is a key resource for managerial decision-making.

With what appears to be a movement toward leading from the heart, why aren't people being trained more formally to use their intuition? Even though there is an increasing number of leaders personally operating in this fashion, there are still many organizations that have invested in IQ and/or EQ training because it's the "safer" way to go.

The more we can clearly define, demystify, and provide practical tools for using intuition, the better. Here are a few takeaways:

How can we practically start exercising our intuition?

What can be done to improve our decision-making from both a personal and business perspective?

- **Respect** your intuition (Remember the times it has served you well).
- **Reflect** on what your intuition is telling you. Follow it and ask questions (Who, what, where, when, why).
- **Project** in community and see what your team members' intuition is telling them. This is how your heart can inform your mind.

We need our heart to lead our head, not the other way around. When we let our intuition inform our intelligence, this is leading from the inside out. As a result, leaders and teams are able to make quicker and more accurate strategic decisions.

A few years ago, my company was gearing up to host a large regional leadership conference. I had the joy of leading a substantial team through a 6-month planning process. The event sold out a week before it was to begin.

But just a few days before the event, I received the worst possible news: One of my friends passed away in a tragic car accident. He was 30 years old, a creative genius, and a brilliant business mind with his entire life ahead of him.

As you can imagine, everyone was in complete shock. His family traveled to the area where the conference was booked, and details of his service were planned right away. Coincidentally, his memorial service ended up being on the exact day of our leadership conference.

How was I supposed to lead?

I found myself in a place where I couldn't even draw on life experience. I'd never gone through anything quite like it. With major leadership decisions looming, I felt alone.

With just a few days before the big event, I felt an urge to set my emotions aside and focus on our overall goal for the conference. A big part of me wanted to reason my way through and shift into 'getting things done' based on the facts and data given to me. My IQ was calling me.

Simultaneously, I began weighing the positive and negative effects I might have on my team during that turbulent time. My EQ was calling me.

It was clearly a tug of war, and I didn't know which direction to choose. IQ, EQ, or a combination of both?

In light of this whirlwind, I disciplined myself and took some much-needed time in silence. It was there that I had an epiphany.

*I can have all the knowledge and awareness of myself and others, but if I don't **lead from my heart**, how effective can I really be?*

Right then and there, I started to grasp the subtle difference between leading from the heart and leading from the head.

Intelligence relates to the ability to understand, whereas leading from the heart is the ability to understand *and* share in the feelings of another— true empathy! This allows for much more powerful leadership.

According to the *2017 Businessolver Workplace Empathy Monitor*:

- Almost one-third of employees (30 percent) don't feel the company they work for is empathetic, and about half (51 percent) feel that organizations and companies as a whole are not empathetic.
- Six out of 10 employees (60 percent) would be willing to take slightly less pay if their employer showed empathy, and 78 percent of employees would leave an employer for equal pay if the other company was empathetic.

In light of my epiphany, I became committed to going into the heart, feeling what others felt, and leading from there.

Talk about being present!

I quickly set up meetings with each core team member who was deeply impacted by the tragedy. I asked how they were feeling, sharing in the shock and heartache of it all. I cried with them and shared my feelings too - a true exchange with a deeper emotional connection. Then, I allowed them to take whatever time they needed before the conference, even letting them know they could skip the conference if they needed to. Even if the conference ended up being totally different from what we'd planned, my core team was still intact.

Some team members did decide to back out of their role in the conference. Outcomes aside, I completely embraced the process. As I talked with each person, I started getting a deeper sense of what to do next. A clear direction solidified, and I knew we would fill the now-vacant roles. Wouldn't you know, I had people step up that never would have filled those roles otherwise? At the conference I was even able to share what happened and how I decided to lead through it.

Now that we've explored personal intuition, let's look at *team* intuition.

Stay in Your Lane

If we want breakthroughs in team dynamics, each team member needs to believe in the power of intuition, overcome the barriers to intuition, and know how it works collectively in shared vision.

By now, we've thoroughly acknowledged that each team member is immensely valuable and should be appreciated through your focused presence, healthy communication, and distinguished honor. We know that each team member has a marked position and a set of responsibilities they bring to the table for their team and its broader vision.

You are the expert in your lane. You carry a wealth of knowledge, experience, wisdom, intellect, creativity, and problem-solving. As you stay focused in your lane, your intuition grows stronger.

In a 2015 study, *The Importance of Starting Right: The Influence of Accurate Intuition on Performance in Salesperson–Customer Interactions,* the following was found:

"Salespeople make two types of judgments about customers in face-to-face interactions: those that are more intuitive and those that are more deliberative. The authors evaluate the influence of accurate intuitive and deliberative judgments on the performance of salespeople. The results reveal that accurate intuitive judgments improve selling performance by enabling

more appropriate initial sales strategies. These judgments not only help increase the effectiveness of salespeople's selling efforts but also reduce the amount of selling time, resulting in improved selling efficiency. However, performance is compromised when inaccurate deliberative judgments follow accurate intuitive judgments. ***The findings also identify different antecedents to judgment accuracy. Intuitive accuracy is influenced by domain-specific experience, similarity to the customer, and empathy for the customer, whereas listening skills and customer orientation influence deliberative accuracy.***"

In other words, our intuitive accuracy sharpens when we stay in our lane. As teams grow in their *trust for one another,* they naturally share more of what their gut is saying. From this place, team leaders can listen to members individually and as a collective. Then, they can discern what they've heard in relationship to the greater vision and their own intuitive nudges.

As mentioned in Chapter 5, this is where the power of 'one body, many parts' comes in! As team members stay in their lane and share their intuitive insights, they build a profound vision.

Team Exercise

Break up into two groups with a big sheet of paper and color markers for each team. Each group comes up with a current challenge within the organization, and each person says what they think their intuition is saying about it. Then, have a group discussion jotting down the overarching insights with different colors representing each insight.

CHAPTER 9
Team Focus for Outcomes that Matter

"A person who aims at nothing is sure to hit it." – Anonymous

WE CAN BUILD AND FOSTER *team trust* all day long, but one of the key factors that sustains that trust is focus.

Foundations for Focus

The average leader has more natural talents than they realize, but if they're not careful, these tremendous strengths can lead them in too many directions. Activity can be a good or bad thing. Focused activity is a great thing!

For example, many businesses have adopted an open floor plan. This brings a sense of community, authenticity, and approachability. In many ways, it has taken down the dividing wall of hierarchy. Yet, it comes at a cost.

To the credit of many businesses that have implemented an open door policy, they do have rules. But unfortunately many of those rules are not enforced.

Team members may put on headphones, but it's just a matter of time before someone taps you on the shoulder and says, "*Got a minute?*" Before long, a minute becomes an hour, and you've been taken down a road you didn't want or need to go down.

How are we to respond to a world that is always tugging at us and demanding our time and attention?

You might be thinking:

"*Robb's Inside Out Leadership is clearly about people before things, so how am I to stay focused?*"

"*Do I set my work aside and talk to every team member who is tapping me on the shoulder?*"

"*Do I say no to every person that comes my way?*"

When we respect our own boundaries, we are living and leading from the inside out.

As a leader grows and develops, others are only going to want more of their time, not less. **It's our management of those demands that sets us up for failure or success.**

It's all about individual and team focus.

Productivity expert and author, Penny Zenker says that distractions are the #1 productivity killer. Studies show we are interrupted 5 times per hour on average, and that 59% of people feel emotionally depleted and mentally distracted. In her book, *The Productivity Zone*, Zenker reveals what she calls The Productivity Curve:

"*This curve determines your level of personal productivity and satisfaction. The ends of the curve are outliers, or extremes. These are areas you want to avoid because the closer you get to them, the more your life is out of balance.*"

It's at those corners where you'll allow yourself to make excuses. The goal is to reach the Productivity Zone where effective and efficient meet.

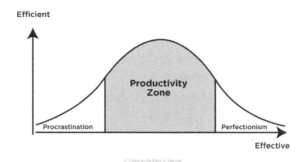

Procrastination

Look at the far left side of the curve. What you see are the people who aren't getting things done; they aren't accomplishing what they want. They're neither efficient nor effective. Maybe they're lacking clarity, or maybe they're stuck in complacency. Maybe they're unconsciously terrified of the very success they say they want. This is the environment that breeds procrastination.

There is a fine line between prioritization and avoidance. Priorities are usually the most important items, not the most urgent ones. A procrastinator's list is upside down, and they focus only on the urgent tasks, leaving the important ones to collect dust. However, it is these important tasks that really need doing, and by ignoring them, procrastinators remain stuck in place.

Perfectionism

Now, consider the far right side of the curve. Those are the people who can't stop doing and doing and doing. They're the perfectionists, or what politically correct people would call "overachievers." Give them some credit: they are effective, they may even make a lot of money, but they are rarely efficient. Many entrepreneurs fall in this category; chances are YOU do too.

There is a fine line, however, between dedication and fixation. When you push and push, there's a breaking point where the price of "one more thing" becomes too great to ignore. Overachievers can get a huge number of things done. Sometimes, people become so addicted to the adrenaline rush and excitement of doing, and get so caught in the overdrive, they forget how to stop. They often forget or ignore their own needs."

One thing I enjoy about Zenker's productivity curve is that it reminds me I'm human. I lean towards perfectionism at times, although I prefer terms like Mover and Shaker and Momentum Guy!

I may bend in that direction at times, but it doesn't mean I have to camp out there. Leading from the inside out is about acknowledging where I'm leaning so I can live and lead more intentionally in the productivity zone.

If you want to see where you land, take Zenker's distraction quiz at: www.distractionquiz.com.

The One Thing Principle

What's the *one thing* that you need to do right now? If you want to be successful, you're going to have to decide on that one thing and do it. Gary Keller in his book *The One Thing* explains the principle:

"What's the ONE Thing you can do such that by doing it everything else will be easier or unnecessary?" Write it down. That's your plan for today. You're allowed to have as many someday goals as you want, but for today, you need to work on just one thing.

At any moment in time there can be only ONE Thing, and when that ONE Thing is in line with your purpose and sits atop your priorities, it will be the most productive thing you can do to launch you toward the best you can be. This simple principle can help you to drop the distracted baggage that you're carrying around, and free you to pursue a single profitable action."

Historically, I have found that writing is something I can get distracted from very easily. A huge part of what I do through my company, Holman International, is to develop new Inside Out Leadership content. Once it is developed, I integrate that new content into my executive coaching, training workshops, and keynote speaking engagements. In other words, my livelihood comes from me churning out content. But what happens when I can't get in a zone because so many things are pulling on me from every direction?

Just as I sit down and try to get into the productivity zone, I get a ping on my phone, a knock at the door, social media updates are flowing in, and my mind is wandering every which way.

Anyone else with me on this?

The *one thing* principle has helped me realize that focus is a choice - one priority at a time. This focus is initiated by having and maintaining self-awareness.

Self-Awareness Helps Us Lead from the Inside Out

In Daniel Goleman's book, *Focus: The Hidden Driver of Excellence*, he explores why people become distracted in the first place.

"The prefrontal cortex of our brain, the outer layer that controls your executive functions - concentrating, planning, and synthesizing - is in a

constant tug-of-war with the deeper, more atavistic [archaic] sector where your impulses arise.

Think of it as a good and bad angel sitting on either shoulder and whispering into your ears.

Once you understand that the primordial part of your brain—the mischievous part—wants you to be distracted, the challenge is to find ways to ignore that dark angel on your shoulder. Every time an urge to switch your attention arises, you need to muster the wherewithal to pull yourself back to the task at hand."

Goleman recommends a simple approach to improving your concentration: Know the 3 basic types of focus - inner, other, and outer.

INNER focus is the ability to listen to your deepest self, your "true north." Who are you, what are your values, why are you doing the work you're doing?

OTHER focus enables us to zero in on what others are saying, thinking, and feeling by not only paying attention to words, but also picking up on nonverbal signals, such as facial expressions and body language.

OUTER focus is the ability to look at what's going on in the world at large, assimilating only what's relevant to your business."

As I began to understand my brain in this way, it gave me more power to overcome distractions. The more my self-awareness grew, the better I became at self-management. The better I became at self-management, the more I grew in team awareness and team management.

It's good to keep these foundational concepts in mind, but it's even better to build upon them. Personally, I began to minimize distractions by consistently leaving my comfortable environment - my home office - and going to a local library. Once I arrived, I knew that half the battle was won, but how to fight the rest? Shut down other distractions like your phone and social media until your time block is over. For me, this is best done by closing all social media tabs, turning my cell phone off, and placing my phone in another room.

In addition, I was on Estie Rand's Business Breakthrough Podcast, and she provided useful insight into this topic. First, she asked how I start my day.

I responded, "by giving thanks, prayer, and exercise." Then she asked when I typically work on new content. I said it was usually early to mid-afternoon. She encouraged me to spend time on my creative content following my early morning routine as my endorphins are high and my creative thoughts are flowing. After that on-air coaching session, I implemented some new habits and made adjustments.

After learning about the Productivity Zone, The One Thing, and self-awareness principles, I implemented these four things:

- I keep in mind my unhealthy leaning on the Productivity Curve so I can take proactive steps to focus.
- I leave my most distracting environment.
- I shut the outside world down while creating content.
- I tap in at the most creative part of the day.

Although I'm still not perfect, my efforts have helped me remain more focused and productive. When I'm with a team member, I'm fully present without other tasks consuming my mind.

As we learn to lead from the inside out, we naturally become more focused ourselves, but there are ways teams can gain focus together too.

Laser Focus—Let's Get Practical!

Distractions are all around us. It's all too easy to follow a career opportunity that sounds good down a rabbit hole, even when it's not the right fit for us. You want to make the best career decision that is also the most efficient use of your time. It's important for you to maintain balance by guarding boundaries.

In order to know your boundaries, you must first understand your priorities in any given season.

Once you clearly define and embrace your priorities, you can sift through opportunities, obligations, and favors through your 'priority lens.'

Remember that each time you say no to something you ought not engage in, you get to say yes to your priorities.

Here is a great evidence-based resource for creating and maintaining healthy boundaries: Before pursuing a new opportunity, I recommend asking these 5 questions:

1. Does it help me achieve my priorities?
2. How much time and effort will this take?
3. Will it help me to gain new skills or improve existing skills?
4. Will this opportunity evolve into something I truly want to do?
5. What is the short-term and long-term payoff?

If your answers to these questions aren't all positive, it might be best to let that opportunity pass.

CHAPTER 10
Transformational Teams Finish Strong

"Winning does not always mean coming in first. Real victory is in arriving at the finish line with no regrets because you know you've gone all out." – Apolo Ohno

YOU PLAN A NEAR PERFECT meeting. Trust seems to be at an all-time high, team focus is clear, and team members leave feeling super energized. But after the meeting, little changes. Why? With never-ending to-do lists, team members get swept back into their crazy routines. Promising new strategies get put on hold. Handouts get lost. Specifics get hazy. In the end, the meeting's value is lost.

Where did the momentum go?

What holds teams back from creating the sustainable momentum they're truly after?

Follow through.

As we have learned, impactful teams build trust from the inside out. However, what good is rock solid trust without leveraging it for a greater purpose?

I have discovered 5 practical things that transformational teams do to ensure good follow through and finish strong.

Evaluation: How a Humble Reality Check Can Make You a Better Team Member

Whether you realize it or not, people pick up on something when you walk into a room. It could be good or bad. It could be excitement, hope, and joy, or worry, anxiety, and doubt.

Effective leadership consistently engages with humble reality checks. One of the best ways to be a valuable team member is to ask those around you how they feel when you're around, how you can better serve, and some ways to boost your leadership.

In Jim Collins' bestselling book, *Good to Great,* he shares the secret of what separates great leaders from good leaders: Great leaders walk in genuine humility.

Ask team members on a regular basis how you can communicate more effectively and provide clearer encouragement. Give them permission to be honest and transparent because effective leadership is all about remaining a student. It requires a humble heart and a strong desire to see people become all that they were created to be. Take a practical step this week and ask a team member these questions. This is how we get closer to igniting team empowerment, as we talked about in Chapter 7.

Demand honesty and be willing to accept that honesty without taking it too personally. I know this takes a level of authenticity and courage, but by now you have enough awareness and practical tools to take this important step.

Can you imagine if each and every team member committed to this level of transparency and honesty on a regular basis with no fear of judgment?

You might be thinking, *"Ok Robb, but what about team evaluation?"*

For personal, team, and organizational evaluation, I encourage people to use the **SWOT analysis** (or SWOT matrix). SWOT is a strategic planning technique used to identify strengths, weaknesses, opportunities, and threats related to business competition and project planning.

I've found that taking the SWOT, both personally and organizationally, is one of the best things a team member can do. Implementing it on a quarterly basis can provide the alignment your team needs to focus and follow through together.

- Fill out the SWOT below and prioritize the items in each box.
- Come back and discuss it as a group.
- Then ask for real results and compare.
- Discuss lessons learned and decide on one area of focus for the next 3 months.

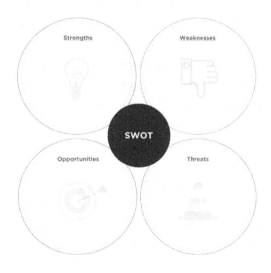

Be honest about *what* you want and *why* you want it.

Once you have an honest evaluation you can share in vision together. Evaluation aligns teams and leaders so they are prepared to focus.

What is a specific goal that your team shares? You want this to be as specific as possible. I am a firm believer that a specific request will yield a specific result.

I am reminded of a few years ago when my wife and I had our sights set on buying a new house. Was that it? No. We had to imagine the house each of us wanted and talk about our visions together. We would look at pictures online and discern which houses we liked and didn't like. Our desires for the size, color, and layout of the inside and outside slowly became clearer. By talking through our personal opinions and thoughts, we arrived at a specific team goal.

We wanted a single family home built in the last 30 years with a small yard in a close-knit neighborhood. This was our *what,* but we needed a *why* to infuse meaning and purpose into the goal.

Our *why* was that we wanted the single-family home to create space for our growing family. I'm 6'4' and my wife is 5'11" - Can you imagine how big our kids will most likely be!? Room to stretch out and relax was important, especially for a highly active family. At the same time, not being too far from others was important because we love community. Getting to know our neighbors and those around us was a priority.

You might say that you want to get a promotion by the end of the year or hit your sales numbers out of the park, but why? Are you on a specific career track and want to hit a milestone before a certain age? Get to the heart of what it is you really want and embrace it.

I've found that when we ask *why* 3 times in a row, going deeper each time we answer, we get down to the core reason for what we want.

Understand the Sacrifice

This is a step that can hurt. It's a step that very few leaders and teams are willing to make. It can be painful, it can be inconvenient, it can be extra hard work, and it can bring with it some blood, sweat, and tears. I call it learning to count the cost together. If your team agrees to the *what* and the *why*, then what will it cost you together? Often, there is a price to be paid at the early stages of a great accomplishment.

Are you All In?

Recently, I had a minor medical procedure. The recovery was uncomfortable, aggravating, and even painful. As a good patient, I followed the doctor's instructions of ice and no regular activity for about a week. For someone like me, it seemed like an eternity! However, I knew the long-term payoff would be absolutely amazing. Just 7 days later, I started feeling much better and was even inspired to go out and do some light activity.

Every act has the potential to take away time or effort that could be committed to something else. This requires a trade-off. Often temporary sacrifice leads to great payoff.

If a team goal is to be more organized, you need to spend time every day maintaining the system you put in place. If your team goal is to boost service to your existing clients, this may require more time calling clients and meeting them face-to-face.

Teams that are All In count the costs and make the necessary sacrifices. Interestingly, you start to realize it wasn't as much of a sacrifice as you initially thought. Short-term pain can yield long-term gain.

Prepare for Success

Nike's *Just Do It* slogan is only one side of the proverbial coin. If a team merely relies on grit, determination, and endurance, the heart of a champion is there, but the mind of a champion may not be. **We need to engage our hearts and our minds for maximum team impact.**

Have you ever heard of the expression, *"Work smarter, not harder?"* This is how teams orchestrate smart and proactive game plans. Whatever your goal is, look at the steps you'll need to take and enlist the tools and people you'll need to get it done. It's a far more effective strategy than relying on sheer willpower.

A business strategy is, in itself, a focused endeavor. In order to form a strategy, you must isolate your end goal, an objective. Then, you must define the path to get there. Your strategy becomes your "one thing" task list. Once you have your strategy, you know exactly what you should be achieving on a daily, weekly, and monthly basis. Your business strategy is a summary of how the company will achieve its goals and meet expectations.

In his article, *Start Strong: Your 100 Day Plan*, Lee Colan says, *"The best way to finish strong is to start strong. That's one reason each new president creates a plan for 'The First 100 Days.' Involve your team in developing this plan."*

I love this brilliant advice. 2 things that will further set you up for success:

- Make sure you have systems in place that can best facilitate your growth. Create systems for as many of your goal-related tasks as possible.
- Make sure you create deadlines for your goals and tasks. Break down the steps and assign a deadline to each, creating a schedule of things that need to be accomplished with the goals and tasks involved (overall goal, outcomes, and tasks under each outcome).

Even if you are not the most detailed person in the world, you can create a simple plan that reaps big team rewards.

Think about vacations. Most people see value in going to a special place with family or friends once or twice per year. If someone sees value in the vacation, your don't have to twist their arm to think about places they want to go or things they want to see—even for the most laid back non-planner. They will passionately plan aspects of the trip and look forward to the destination.

It comes back to seeing value, together, in what you are doing and why you are doing it - and knowing the costs. Once people are All In, implementing the plan becomes much easier.

Accountability Accelerates Performance

The American Society of Training and Development (ASTD) conducted a study on accountability and found that a person has a 65% chance of completing a goal if they commit to someone. And if you have a specific accountability appointment with a person you've committed to, you will increase your chances of success by up to 95%.

If accountability is such a beneficial thing, why does it have such a bad name?

The reason is simple: Many teams have not seen it modeled well.

Typically, accountability is when someone meets with a team member regularly to point out things they can improve upon. Of course, all of this is in the name of maximizing performance, right? Talk about a nice slap on the wrist!

Instead, what if we not only saw the mutual benefit of accountability, but also redefined how teams experience it?

What if we enlisted colleagues and team members to engage in a form of accountability that sincerely pointed out the good we're doing? This requires much more time spent on genuine uplifting - time spent cultivating encouragement, inspiration, and empowerment. In the midst of this process, we can also tackle some of the obstacles that are getting in the way or holding you back from staying on task and building momentum.

Did you catch the difference? If we rush into what's not getting done, we bypass the chance to build each other up. The former focuses on the problem, and the latter focuses on the good while removing any barriers to progress.

This goes back to the point made in Chapter 7 by Demarest: "When you are value-centric, it's not all about you; it's about adding value, period. Your intention is to create the greatest possible net value for everyone, including yourself."

As we intentionally seek out accountability, we come full circle. What an opportunity to be present and foster trust from the inside out!

Reflection Exercise

It's time to enlist friends or colleagues in the process! This will help keep you accountable to the promises you make to yourself and others - *follow-through.*

1. Who is one team member you can enlist to help you stay accountable? If you already have someone, you are one step ahead!
2. Call an initial meeting with a team member to discuss how you can best hold one another accountable and how often you should meet. Mark it down as though you are meeting with your most important client!
3. Keep track in an 'encouragement journal.' Let the good personal and professional reports rule your accountability meetings together. (eg. key victories, gratitude, positive reports, etc.).

CONCLUSION

THERE HAS NEVER BEEN A person just like you, there isn't a person just like you now, and there will never be another person just like you on planet earth. Embrace your uniqueness!

As amazing as this is, if we're not careful, we will naturally surround ourselves with people that look like us, sound like us, and validate our own opinions and thoughts.

All In is about learning how to embrace our uniqueness only to embrace others who are different.

When you are committed to building trust from the inside out with team members who are different from you, a transformation occurs within ourselves and with those in our sphere of influence!

Think of it like this:

You have finally booked your dream home for your annual vacation getaway and have invited some of your extended family members. How exciting!

After doing extensive research, you landed on a house that has great curb appeal and is even more beautiful and luxurious inside. It has an open concept and multiple rooms to accommodate your entire family.

The big day has finally arrived. The only problem is, when you and your extended family arrive you can't find the master key to open the front door. You were told the key would be under the front door mat, but it's not.

You lead the charge, rallying your family to help find the missing key, but to no avail. Frustration is mounting and tension is building as everyone just wants to get inside.

After nearly an hour, you finally find the key in some bushes on the side of the house. You rush over to unlock the front door and your entire family follows.

You and your family are All In!

The house represents your organization. Your family represents your team members. The front door represents transformational leadership. The key represents trust. You represent the team leader!

All In is my gift to you, the leader.

You now hold the key of trust in your hand and have unlocked the front door of your team and organization.

Be encouraged that the key of trust has the power to strengthen, sharpen, and unify the most diverse team.

Before opening this gift, maybe you were on the outside looking in? Perhaps you were looking for other keys that were not opening the door?

Now *All In* has given you access to the areas that build lasting team success:

1. Building Trust that Lasts
2. Communications: What's in It for Them Is What's in It for You
3. Embracing the Story
4. Team Dynamics for a Dynamic Team
5. Developing a Culture of Honor
6. Turning Conflict into a Creative Superpower
7. Igniting Team Empowerment
8. Team Intuition: Where Breakthroughs Happen

9. Team Focus for Outcomes that Matter
10. Transformational Teams Finish Strong

When we gain access and remain committed to all the rooms in the house, this is how impactful teams build trust from the inside out and go **All In!**

Learn More...

Robb Holman is an internationally recognized leadership keynote speaker and trainer who helps audiences connect with their unique life purpose and find success in a way they never expected - from the inside out!

If you're interested in having Robb give a passionate keynote talk or experiential training workshop on *All In,* or learning more about his Inside Out Leadership™ products and services, visit:

www.robbholman.com

Robb's Books:

Lead the Way: *Inside Out Leadership™ Principles for Business* Owners & Leaders
www.LeadTheWayBook.com

All In: *How Impactful Teams Build Trust From the Inside Out*
www.GetAllInBook.com

Robb's Inside Out Leadership™ Academy:

www.InsideOutLeadershipAcademy.com

To interact with Robb, visit:

Twitter: **www.twitter.com/robbholman**
Facebook: **www.facebook.com/robbholman1**
LinkedIn: **www.linkedin.com/in/robbholman**
YouTube: **www.youtube.com/c/robbholman**
Instagram: **www.instagram.com/robb.holman**

POSITIVE. PASSIONATE. POWERFUL.

RH ROBB HOLMAN
INSIDE OUT LEADERSHIP

ROBB HOLMAN

is an internationally recognized leadership expert, executive coach, keynote speaker, podcast co-host, and bestselling author who has a heart for authentic relationships and a true talent for equipping people with the skills and the knowledge necessary for their success. His work has been featured in top publications like Inc., Forbes, and Fast Company and endorsed by many of the world's top leadership thinkers.

http://www.robbholman.com/speaking

 Robb.holman

 Robbholman1

 Robbholman

 @Robbholman

 www.robbholman.com

 484.401.7966

 info@robbholman.com

> *Robb is a charismatic and dynamic speaker who has the ability to capture an audience from the moment he speaks. You can tell by his presence the passion he has for his business and his leadership. I would highly recommend Robb for any speaking engagements. The take-away knowledge and inspiration for your audience is abundant.*
>
> **— Carla Haydt**

ABOUT THE BOOK

Internationally recognized leadership expert reveals his secrets for lasting leadership success to help you LEAD the WAY.

http://leadthewaybook.com/

To Purchase the book go to .com

www.robbholman.com

484.401.7966

info@robbholman.com